NEURAL NETWORK PROGRAMMING

HOW TO CREATE MODERN AI SYSTEMS WITH PYTHON, TENSORFLOW, AND KERAS

4 BOOKS IN 1

BOOK 1
NEURAL NETWORK PROGRAMMING FOR BEGINNERS: BUILDING AI SYSTEMS WITH PYTHON, TENSORFLOW, AND KERAS FROM SCRATCH

BOOK 2
ADVANCED NEURAL NETWORK PROGRAMMING: MASTERING DEEP LEARNING TECHNIQUES WITH PYTHON, TENSORFLOW, AND KERAS

BOOK 3
NEURAL NETWORK PROGRAMMING: BEYOND THE BASICS: EXPLORING ADVANCED CONCEPTS AND ARCHITECTURES FOR AI WITH PYTHON, TENSORFLOW, AND KERAS

BOOK 4
EXPERT NEURAL NETWORK PROGRAMMING: PUSHING THE BOUNDARIES OF AI DEVELOPMENT WITH ADVANCED PYTHON, TENSORFLOW, AND KERAS TECHNIQUES

ROB BOTWRIGHT

Published by Rob Botwright
Library of Congress Cataloging-in-Publication Data
ISBN 978-1-83938-644-2
Cover design by Rizzo

Disclaimer

The contents of this book are based on extensive research and the best available historical sources. However, the author and publisher make no claims, promises, or guarantees about the accuracy, completeness, or adequacy of the information contained herein. The information in this book is provided on an "as is" basis, and the author and publisher disclaim any and all liability for any errors, omissions, or inaccuracies in the information or for any actions taken in reliance on such information. The opinions and views expressed in this book are those of the author and do not necessarily reflect the official policy or position of any organization or individual mentioned in this book. Any reference to specific people, places, or events is intended only to provide historical context and is not intended to defame or malign any group, individual, or entity. The information in this book is intended for educational and entertainment purposes only. It is not intended to be a substitute for professional advice or judgment. Readers are encouraged to conduct their own research and to seek professional advice where appropriate. Every effort has been made to obtain necessary permissions and acknowledgments for all images and other copyrighted material used in this book. Any errors or omissions in this regard are unintentional, and the author and publisher will correct them in future editions.

Introduction

Welcome to "Neural Network Programming: How to Create Modern AI Systems with Python, TensorFlow, and Keras," a comprehensive bundle that will take you on an exciting journey into the fascinating world of artificial intelligence and deep learning. Within the pages of these four meticulously crafted books, you will embark on a learning adventure that spans from the fundamentals of neural networks to the cutting-edge techniques that drive the future of AI development.

In this era of technological advancement, artificial intelligence has emerged as a transformative force, revolutionizing industries and reshaping our daily lives. From self-driving cars and virtual personal assistants to medical diagnostics and financial predictions, AI is at the heart of these groundbreaking innovations. Neural networks, in particular, have played a pivotal role in this AI revolution, enabling machines to learn, adapt, and make decisions akin to human intelligence.

This book bundle is designed to cater to a diverse audience, ranging from absolute beginners with no prior AI experience to seasoned professionals looking to push the boundaries of AI development. Each book in this series is carefully structured to provide a step-by-step progression of knowledge, ensuring that readers of all backgrounds can benefit and grow their expertise.

Let's take a closer look at what each book in this bundle has to offer:
Book 1 - Neural Network Programming for Beginners: Building AI Systems with Python, TensorFlow, and Keras from Scratch This book serves as your entry point into the world of neural networks. We start from the ground up, introducing you to the basics of artificial intelligence and guiding you through Python programming. As you immerse yourself in the world of TensorFlow and Keras, you will learn to build AI systems from scratch, gaining hands-on experience in creating and training your neural networks.

Book 2 - Advanced Neural Network Programming: Mastering Deep Learning Techniques with Python, TensorFlow, and Keras Building on the foundation established in Book 1, this volume takes you deeper into the realm of deep learning. You will explore advanced techniques, fine-tune models, and master the intricacies of TensorFlow and Keras. With a focus on real-world applications and projects, you'll be equipped to tackle complex AI challenges and drive innovation in your field.

Book 3 - Neural Network Programming: Beyond the Basics: Exploring Advanced Concepts and Architectures for AI with Python, TensorFlow, and Keras In this book, we transcend the fundamentals, delving into advanced concepts and cutting-edge architectures. From Convolutional Neural Networks (CNNs) to Generative Adversarial Networks (GANs), you will explore the full spectrum of neural network possibilities. This book empowers you to craft innovative AI solutions and opens doors to exciting AI research.

Book 4 - Expert Neural Network Programming: Pushing the Boundaries of AI Development with Advanced Python, TensorFlow, and Keras Techniques Our final volume is designed for those who aspire to become experts in the field of neural network programming. We explore quantum neural networks, ethical AI, model deployment, and gaze into the future of AI research and development. With advanced Python, TensorFlow, and Keras techniques at your disposal, you will push the boundaries of AI development and contribute to the forefront of AI innovation.

Whether you are an aspiring AI enthusiast, a seasoned developer, a researcher, or a professional seeking to stay at the cutting edge of AI technology, this book bundle offers something for everyone. Prepare to embark on a transformative journey through the realms of neural network programming, as we equip you with the knowledge, skills, and tools to create modern AI systems that will shape the future.

So, without further ado, let's dive into the world of neural network programming and discover the limitless possibilities of artificial intelligence.

BOOK 1
NEURAL NETWORK PROGRAMMING FOR BEGINNERS:
BUILDING AI SYSTEMS WITH PYTHON, TENSORFLOW,
AND KERAS FROM SCRATCH

ROB BOTWRIGHT

Chapter 1: Introduction to Neural Networks

The history and evolution of neural networks trace back to the mid-20th century, when researchers first began developing artificial neural networks inspired by the human brain's structure and function. These early neural networks were simple and had limited capabilities compared to today's sophisticated models. One of the earliest significant developments in neural network history was the creation of the perceptron in the late 1950s by Frank Rosenblatt. The perceptron was a single-layer neural network designed for binary classification tasks. Although it was a pioneering effort, the perceptron had limitations, and it could only solve linearly separable problems.

The field of neural networks experienced a period of stagnation and reduced interest in the 1960s and 1970s due to the perceptron's limitations and the absence of effective training algorithms for multilayer networks. It wasn't until the 1980s that neural networks experienced a resurgence in popularity, thanks to advancements in training algorithms and the development of backpropagation, which allowed for the training of multi-layer networks.

In the 1980s and 1990s, neural networks found applications in various fields, including pattern recognition, speech recognition, and image processing. However, their capabilities were still limited by the computing resources available at the time, and they were often outperformed by traditional machine learning techniques.

The late 1990s and early 2000s saw the rise of support vector machines (SVMs) and other machine learning algorithms, which overshadowed neural networks in many applications. During this period, neural networks were less prevalent in the machine learning landscape.

The turning point for neural networks came in the mid-2000s with the advent of deep learning. Deep learning is a subfield of machine learning that focuses on training deep neural networks with multiple hidden layers. These deep neural networks, often referred to as deep neural networks or deep learning models, demonstrated remarkable performance improvements in various domains, including image recognition, natural language processing, and speech recognition.

One of the pivotal moments in the history of deep learning was the 2012 ImageNet competition, where a deep convolutional neural network (CNN) known as AlexNet achieved a significant reduction in error rates, outperforming all other competitors. This breakthrough demonstrated the potential of deep neural networks and ignited widespread interest and investment in deep learning research.

The subsequent years witnessed rapid advancements in neural network architectures, optimization techniques, and hardware acceleration. Researchers developed various types of neural networks, such as recurrent neural networks (RNNs) for sequential data and long short-term memory networks (LSTMs) for handling vanishing gradient problems in deep networks.

The availability of powerful graphics processing units (GPUs) and specialized hardware like tensor processing units (TPUs) further accelerated the training of deep neural networks, making it feasible to train large-scale models with billions of parameters.

With the rise of deep learning, neural networks achieved state-of-the-art performance in numerous applications. In natural language processing, recurrent neural networks and transformers, such as BERT and GPT-3, achieved remarkable results in tasks like machine translation, text generation, and sentiment analysis. In computer vision, convolutional neural networks revolutionized image classification, object detection, and image segmentation.

Neural networks have also made significant contributions in healthcare, aiding in medical image analysis, disease diagnosis, and drug discovery. They have found applications in autonomous vehicles, robotics, finance, and recommendation systems, among many other domains.

The evolution of neural networks continues, with ongoing research and development focused on improving model interpretability, robustness, and efficiency. Efforts are being made to address ethical concerns related to bias and fairness in AI algorithms, ensuring that neural networks are used responsibly and ethically.

In summary, the history and evolution of neural networks have been marked by periods of growth, stagnation, and resurgence. From the early days of perceptrons to the deep learning revolution, neural networks have evolved into powerful tools with a broad range of applications. Their future holds promise as researchers continue to push the boundaries of what neural networks can achieve, making them a cornerstone of modern artificial intelligence.

To understand neural network programming, it's essential to grasp some key concepts that underpin the field. At the core of neural networks are artificial neurons, also known as nodes or units. These neurons mimic the functionality of biological neurons and are the building blocks of neural networks.

Each artificial neuron takes multiple inputs, applies a mathematical operation to them, and produces an output. The output is determined by a combination of weights and biases associated with the neuron. Weights represent the strength of connections between neurons, while biases provide an offset to the output.

The weighted sum of inputs and biases is then passed through an activation function, which introduces non-linearity into the network. Activation functions play a crucial role in allowing neural networks to model complex relationships in data.

There are several common activation functions used in neural networks, including the sigmoid function, hyperbolic tangent (tanh), and rectified linear unit (ReLU). Each activation function has its properties and use cases. Sigmoid and tanh functions squash their input into a specific range, while ReLU provides a simple thresholding operation.

Neurons in a neural network are organized into layers. The three primary types of layers are the input layer, hidden layers, and the output layer. The input layer receives the initial data, while the hidden layers process and transform the data through various intermediate representations. The output layer produces the final results or predictions.

The connections between neurons in different layers are characterized by weights. During training, these weights are adjusted to minimize the difference between the network's predictions and the actual target values. This process is known as supervised learning and involves the use of a loss function to quantify the prediction error.

A widely used loss function in various applications is the mean squared error (MSE), which measures the average squared difference between predicted and actual values. Other loss functions, such as cross-entropy, are used in classification tasks.

Training a neural network typically involves optimization algorithms, such as gradient descent, which update weights to minimize the loss function. Gradient descent iteratively adjusts weights in the direction that reduces the loss, making the network's predictions more accurate.

In deep learning, neural networks with multiple hidden layers are referred to as deep neural networks (DNNs). These networks can capture complex patterns and hierarchies in data, enabling them to excel in tasks such as image recognition, natural language processing, and game playing.

Convolutional neural networks (CNNs) are a specialized type of neural network commonly used for image analysis. They apply convolutional operations to capture spatial patterns in images, reducing the number of parameters and improving the network's ability to recognize objects.

Recurrent neural networks (RNNs) are designed to handle sequential data. They have connections that loop back on themselves, allowing them to maintain internal states and process sequences of varying lengths. RNNs are used in tasks like speech recognition and language modeling.

Long Short-Term Memory networks (LSTMs) and Gated Recurrent Units (GRUs) are variants of RNNs that address the vanishing gradient problem. They are well-suited for modeling long-range dependencies in sequential data.

Transformers are a breakthrough architecture in natural language processing. They use self-attention mechanisms to process input sequences in parallel, making them highly efficient and effective in tasks like machine translation and text generation.

Regularization techniques are crucial for preventing overfitting in neural networks. Methods like dropout randomly deactivate a fraction of neurons during training, reducing the network's reliance on specific connections and improving its generalization.

Batch normalization is another technique that normalizes the input to each layer, stabilizing training and accelerating convergence. Weight regularization methods, such as L1 and L2 regularization, add penalties to the loss function to discourage large weight values.

Transfer learning leverages pre-trained neural network models on large datasets. By fine-tuning these models for specific tasks, transfer learning allows developers to achieve state-of-the-art results with limited data.

Neural network programming often involves libraries and frameworks like TensorFlow, Keras, PyTorch, and scikit-learn. These tools provide high-level abstractions, making it easier to design, train, and evaluate neural networks.

In practice, neural network programming also requires data preprocessing and exploration. Data must be cleaned, transformed, and split into training, validation, and test sets to ensure reliable model performance assessment.

Hyperparameter tuning is an essential step in optimizing neural networks. Hyperparameters, such as learning rates, batch sizes, and network architectures, are adjusted to find the best configuration for a given task.

Interpreting neural networks and understanding their decision-making processes are active areas of research. Techniques like saliency maps and feature visualization help shed light on what factors influence a model's predictions.

Neural network programming extends beyond the technical aspects, as ethical considerations are increasingly important. Ensuring fairness, transparency, and bias mitigation in AI systems is essential for responsible deployment.

The field of neural network programming continues to evolve rapidly, with ongoing research pushing the boundaries of what these models can achieve. As technology advances, neural networks are likely to play an increasingly prominent role in solving complex problems across various domains.

Chapter 2: Setting Up Your Development Environment

Selecting the appropriate Integrated Development Environment (IDE) and tools is a crucial step in any software development project, including neural network programming. The choice you make can significantly impact your productivity, code quality, and overall development experience.

The first consideration when choosing an IDE is the programming language you intend to use for your neural network projects. Popular languages for deep learning include Python, R, and Julia, each with its set of IDEs and libraries. Python, in particular, is widely adopted in the machine learning community, and many specialized IDEs are available for it.

For Python-based neural network programming, one of the most popular IDEs is PyCharm. PyCharm provides a powerful environment for Python development, offering features such as code completion, debugging tools, and integration with popular neural network libraries like TensorFlow and PyTorch.

Another popular option for Python development is Jupyter Notebook. Jupyter Notebook is an interactive environment that allows you to create and share documents containing live code, equations, visualizations, and narrative text. It's an excellent choice for exploring and prototyping machine learning and neural network code.

Visual Studio Code (VS Code) is a highly extensible and lightweight IDE that supports various programming languages, including Python. VS Code's extensive marketplace offers numerous extensions for neural network development, making it a versatile choice for deep learning projects.

If you prefer an IDE with a specific focus on data science and machine learning, consider using tools like Anaconda and JupyterLab. Anaconda is a Python distribution that comes with many pre-installed data science packages and libraries, making it easy to set up a development environment. JupyterLab is an advanced Jupyter Notebook interface that provides a more feature-rich and flexible coding experience.

Beyond Python-specific IDEs, there are also cloud-based development environments tailored for machine learning. Google Colab and Kaggle Kernels are examples of cloud-based platforms that allow you to run Python code with access to powerful GPUs and TPUs, making them suitable for training deep learning models without needing dedicated hardware.

If you prefer using R for your neural network projects, RStudio is the IDE of choice. RStudio offers a comprehensive environment for R programming, data analysis, and machine learning, with built-in support for R's neural network libraries and packages.

For those exploring Julia for deep learning, the JuliaPro IDE is a suitable option. JuliaPro provides a user-friendly environment for Julia development, with support for libraries like Flux.jl, an increasingly popular choice for neural network programming in Julia.

Regardless of your language choice, it's essential to consider the availability of libraries and packages for neural network development. TensorFlow and PyTorch are two of the most widely used deep learning frameworks, with extensive communities and resources available for both. The IDE you choose should seamlessly integrate with these frameworks and provide tools for model visualization and debugging.

When selecting an IDE, you should also consider your workflow and preferences. Some developers prefer a lightweight text editor, such as Sublime Text or Atom, combined with command-line tools for neural network programming. These editors can be customized with extensions and plugins to suit your specific needs.

Another aspect to evaluate is the IDE's support for version control systems like Git. Effective version control is essential for collaborating on neural network projects and tracking changes over time. IDEs like PyCharm and VS Code have built-in Git integration, simplifying the version control process.

Collaboration tools are another consideration, particularly if you are working on neural network projects with a team. Platforms like GitHub, GitLab, and Bitbucket provide hosting for code repositories, issue tracking, and collaboration features that facilitate teamwork and project management.

Additionally, cloud-based machine learning platforms like Amazon SageMaker, Google Cloud AI Platform, and Microsoft Azure Machine Learning offer integrated development environments and tools tailored for building and deploying machine learning models at scale. These platforms provide a comprehensive ecosystem for neural network development, including data preprocessing, model training, and deployment capabilities.

Choosing the right IDE and tools ultimately depends on your specific needs, project requirements, and personal preferences. Whether you opt for a language-specific IDE like PyCharm or RStudio, a versatile text editor like VS Code, or a cloud-based platform like Google Colab, your selection should align with your neural network programming goals and provide the necessary support for efficient development and experimentation. Before diving into neural network programming, it's essential to have the right tools and libraries installed and properly configured on your development environment. Next, we will walk through the process of installing and configuring TensorFlow and Keras, two of the most popular deep learning frameworks for Python.

To get started, you'll need to have Python installed on your system. Python is the primary programming language used in deep learning, and it serves as the foundation for TensorFlow and Keras.

You can download Python from the official Python website (python.org) and follow the installation instructions for your specific operating system.

Once Python is installed, it's a good practice to create a virtual environment for your deep learning projects. Virtual environments allow you to isolate your project's dependencies, ensuring that they do not interfere with other Python packages on your system.

To create a virtual environment, open your command-line interface and run the following command:

Copy code

```
python -m venv myenv
```

Replace "myenv" with the name you want to give to your virtual environment. This command will create a new directory with the specified name, containing a clean Python environment.

To activate the virtual environment, use the following command on Windows:

Copy code

```
myenv\Scripts\activate
```

Or use this command on macOS and Linux:

bashCopy code

```
source myenv/bin/activate
```

With the virtual environment activated, you can now proceed to install TensorFlow and Keras. TensorFlow is an open-source deep learning framework developed by Google, while Keras is a high-level neural networks API that runs on top of TensorFlow.

To install TensorFlow and Keras, use the Python package manager, pip, by running the following command:

Copy code

```
pip install tensorflow keras
```

This command will download and install the latest versions of TensorFlow and Keras along with their dependencies. Make sure your virtual environment is activated when running this command to ensure that the packages are installed within the isolated environment.

Once the installation is complete, you can verify that TensorFlow and Keras are installed correctly by opening a Python interactive session within your virtual environment and importing the libraries:

pythonCopy code

```
import tensorflow as tf import keras print("TensorFlow version:", tf.__version__) print("Keras version:", keras.__version__)
```

These commands should display the versions of TensorFlow and Keras that were installed. This step helps ensure that the libraries are accessible and operational within your virtual environment.

Now that TensorFlow and Keras are successfully installed, you can start configuring your development environment for deep learning tasks. One important consideration is the choice of a backend for Keras.

Keras can use different deep learning frameworks as its backend, with TensorFlow being the most common choice. However, you can configure Keras to use other backends such as Microsoft Cognitive Toolkit (CNTK) or Theano if your project requires it.

To set TensorFlow as the backend for Keras, you can create a Keras configuration file. In your project directory, create a file named "keras.json" with the following content:

jsonCopy code

```
{ "image_data_format": "channels_last", "epsilon": 1e-07, "floatx": "float32", "backend": "tensorflow" }
```

This configuration file specifies that Keras should use TensorFlow as the backend. You can customize other settings in this file to match your project's requirements.

Now, when you import Keras in your Python code, it will automatically use TensorFlow as the backend. This configuration simplifies the setup and allows you to seamlessly switch between different deep learning frameworks if needed.

In addition to configuring the backend, you may want to adjust TensorFlow's GPU support settings if you have a compatible GPU on your machine. Utilizing GPU acceleration can significantly speed up training deep neural networks.

TensorFlow supports both CUDA and cuDNN, which are GPU libraries developed by NVIDIA. To enable GPU support, you'll need to install the GPU version of TensorFlow, which includes these libraries. You can install the GPU version using pip with the following command:
Copy code

```
pip install tensorflow-gpu
```

Ensure that you have the necessary NVIDIA drivers and CUDA toolkit installed on your system before using TensorFlow with GPU support.

Once TensorFlow GPU is installed, you can check if your GPU is recognized by TensorFlow by running the following Python code:
pythonCopy code

```
from tensorflow.python.client import device_lib
print(device_lib.list_local_devices())
```

This code will display information about the available devices, including your GPU if it's correctly configured and recognized.

To take full advantage of GPU acceleration, make sure to adjust your neural network code to utilize the GPU when training models. TensorFlow will automatically use the GPU for computation when available, but you can further optimize GPU memory usage and performance based on your specific requirements. In summary, installing and configuring TensorFlow and Keras is a fundamental step in preparing your development environment for neural network programming. By following these instructions, you can ensure that you have the necessary tools and libraries in place to begin building and training deep learning models efficiently.

Chapter 3: Python Fundamentals for AI

Python serves as the foundation for neural network programming, and before diving into more complex topics, it's essential to understand the basics of Python and its syntax. Python is an interpreted, high-level programming language known for its simplicity and readability. Python uses a straightforward syntax that emphasizes code readability and reduces the cost of program maintenance.

One of the most basic elements in Python is the variable, which is used to store data. Variables can hold various types of data, such as numbers, text, and more complex structures like lists and dictionaries.

In Python, variables are assigned values using the "=" operator, for example: **x = 5** assigns the value 5 to the variable **x**.

Python supports different data types, including integers, floating-point numbers, strings, lists, and dictionaries. You can perform various operations on these data types, such as arithmetic calculations on numbers and string manipulation.

Python uses indentation to define code blocks, unlike many other programming languages that use curly braces or other symbols. Indentation helps maintain a clean and readable code structure, making it a distinctive feature of Python.

Control structures, such as loops and conditional statements, are essential for controlling the flow of a

Python program. The "if" statement allows you to execute code conditionally based on a specified condition.

For example, you can write an "if" statement like this: **if x > 10:** followed by an indented block of code that runs only if the condition **x > 10** is true.

Python provides various types of loops, including the "for" loop and the "while" loop. The "for" loop is used to iterate over sequences like lists and strings, executing a block of code for each item in the sequence.

The "while" loop, on the other hand, continues executing a block of code as long as a specified condition remains true. Loops are fundamental for repetitive tasks and iteration in Python programs.

Functions are reusable blocks of code that can be defined and called multiple times throughout a Python program. Functions help organize code into manageable and modular components, making it easier to understand and maintain.

To define a function in Python, use the "def" keyword, followed by the function name and a set of parentheses that can contain parameters. For example: **def my_function(x, y):**.

Inside the function's block, you write the code that the function will execute when called. Functions can return values using the "return" statement, and these return values can be assigned to variables or used in other parts of your code.

Comments are essential for documenting your Python code, providing explanations and context for both yourself and others who may read your code. Python supports both single-line comments, denoted by the "#" symbol,

and multi-line comments enclosed in triple quotes ("' or
""").

For example, you can write a single-line comment like this:
 # This is a comment. or a multi-line comment as follows:

pythonCopy code

''' This is a multi-line comment. It can span multiple lines.
'''

Python's built-in libraries and modules expand its
functionality, allowing you to perform a wide range of
tasks without reinventing the wheel. You can import these
modules using the "import" keyword.

For example, you can import the "math" module to access
mathematical functions: **import math**.

Once imported, you can use functions and objects from
the module in your code by prefixing them with the
module name, like **math.sqrt(25)** to calculate the square
root of 25.

Python also supports object-oriented programming (OOP),
allowing you to define and use classes and objects. Classes
are blueprints for creating objects, and objects are
instances of a class that encapsulate data and behavior.

Inheritance, encapsulation, and polymorphism are some
of the fundamental concepts of OOP in Python, enabling
you to create more organized and modular code.

Error handling in Python is managed through try-except
blocks, which allow you to handle exceptions and errors
gracefully. The "try" block contains code that might raise
an exception, and the "except" block specifies how to
handle that exception.

This error handling mechanism helps prevent program
crashes and provides an opportunity to recover gracefully
from unexpected issues.

Python's standard library includes a wealth of modules that simplify various tasks. For example, the "os" module provides functions for interacting with the operating system, while the "datetime" module helps with date and time manipulation.

You can explore and leverage these modules to streamline your neural network programming projects and reduce the amount of code you need to write from scratch.

String manipulation is a fundamental skill in Python programming, and the language offers extensive support for working with strings. You can concatenate strings, extract substrings, format text, and perform many other operations with ease.

Lists and dictionaries are two commonly used data structures in Python. Lists are ordered collections of items, while dictionaries are key-value pairs. These data structures are versatile and can be used to store and manipulate data efficiently.

Python's simplicity and readability make it an excellent choice for both beginners and experienced programmers. Its extensive community and rich ecosystem of libraries and frameworks make it a powerful tool for various applications, including neural network programming.

Understanding Python basics and its syntax is essential as you embark on your journey into neural network programming. With a solid foundation in Python, you'll be well-equipped to explore the world of deep learning, machine learning, and artificial intelligence, building sophisticated models and solving complex problems in the field.

NumPy, short for "Numerical Python," is a fundamental

library for numerical computing in Python and plays a crucial role in data manipulation for artificial intelligence (AI) applications. It provides support for large, multi-dimensional arrays and matrices, along with a vast collection of high-level mathematical functions for performing operations on these arrays.

To use NumPy in your Python projects, you need to import it into your code using the "import" command: **import numpy as np**. This common alias, "np," simplifies referencing NumPy functions and objects in your code.

At the core of NumPy is the NumPy array, or simply ndarray, which is a multi-dimensional container for homogeneous data. These arrays are highly efficient, allowing for efficient storage and computation of large datasets, making them a crucial component in AI and machine learning workflows.

You can create a NumPy array from a Python list or other iterable data types. For example, **my_array = np.array([1, 2, 3, 4, 5])** creates a one-dimensional array from a Python list.

NumPy arrays can have multiple dimensions. For instance, you can create a two-dimensional array using a nested list: **my_2d_array = np.array([[1, 2, 3], [4, 5, 6]])**.

Manipulating NumPy arrays is essential for data preprocessing in AI projects. You can perform element-wise operations, such as addition, subtraction, multiplication, and division, on arrays, making it easy to process and transform data.

Broadcasting is a powerful feature in NumPy that allows arrays of different shapes to be combined in a way that makes sense. For example, you can add a scalar value to an entire array or perform operations on arrays with different dimensions.

NumPy provides various methods for array manipulation, including reshaping, slicing, and indexing. These operations allow you to extract specific data subsets, change the shape of arrays, and perform complex data transformations.

In AI applications, handling missing data is a common challenge. NumPy provides tools to work with missing or NaN (Not-a-Number) values, allowing you to identify, replace, or remove them from your datasets.

Statistical analysis is a fundamental component of AI projects, and NumPy offers a wide range of statistical functions to help you analyze data. You can compute mean, median, standard deviation, and other statistical measures easily using NumPy.

Another essential aspect of data manipulation is sorting and searching. NumPy provides functions for sorting arrays along specific axes and searching for elements or conditions within arrays, making it efficient to find relevant data points in large datasets.

NumPy also supports linear algebra operations, such as matrix multiplication, eigenvalue decomposition, and singular value decomposition. These capabilities are valuable for AI tasks like dimensionality reduction and feature extraction.

Random number generation is a critical component in AI applications, and NumPy includes a robust random number generation library. You can generate random data samples, shuffle arrays, and create random matrices for various purposes, such as data augmentation and simulation.

NumPy's integration with other data science libraries, such as pandas and Matplotlib, enhances its capabilities for data manipulation and visualization. Combining NumPy with these libraries allows you to create end-to-end data processing pipelines and generate insightful visualizations.

Data normalization and scaling are common preprocessing steps in AI, and NumPy provides functions to standardize data, rescale values, and normalize data between specific ranges. These operations help ensure that your data is suitable for training AI models.

In AI and machine learning, splitting datasets into training, validation, and test sets is essential for model development and evaluation. NumPy's array manipulation features make it straightforward to split data into these subsets while maintaining data integrity.

NumPy's memory management and data storage efficiency are particularly important when working with large datasets. It allows you to minimize memory usage while optimizing performance, a crucial consideration for AI projects that involve substantial data processing.

Parallel and distributed computing is a growing trend in AI, and NumPy can leverage multi-core processors for parallel processing, enhancing the speed and scalability of your AI workflows.

NumPy's robust library ecosystem extends its capabilities for AI and data manipulation. For instance, SciPy builds on NumPy and offers additional scientific computing functions, including optimization, interpolation, and integration.

Machine learning frameworks like scikit-learn rely on NumPy arrays as their input data format, making NumPy an integral part of the machine learning ecosystem. This compatibility simplifies data preparation and integration with machine learning models.

NumPy's support for custom data types and structured arrays allows you to work with complex data structures efficiently. You can define your data types to represent structured information, making it easier to manipulate and analyze real-world datasets.

In summary, NumPy is a fundamental library for data manipulation in AI and machine learning projects. Its efficient array handling, mathematical functions, and integration with other data science libraries make it a versatile tool for preprocessing, analyzing, and preparing data for AI modeling and deployment. Understanding NumPy and its capabilities is essential for anyone working in the field of artificial intelligence.

Chapter 4: Understanding TensorFlow Basics

In the realm of artificial intelligence and neural network programming, tensors and operations are foundational concepts that form the basis for representing and manipulating data. A tensor, at its core, is a multi-dimensional array with a uniform type. Tensors come in various forms, from scalars (0-dimensional tensors) representing single values to multi-dimensional arrays capable of storing and processing complex data structures.

Tensors are fundamental for neural networks, as they serve as the primary data structures for input data, model parameters, and outputs. In Python, libraries like NumPy provide efficient tensor support, allowing you to work with tensors seamlessly.

The dimensionality of a tensor determines its rank. A scalar has a rank of 0, a vector (1-dimensional array) has a rank of 1, a matrix (2-dimensional array) has a rank of 2, and so on. Understanding tensor ranks is essential because they dictate the number of indices required to access elements within the tensor.

Tensors can have different shapes, which describe their sizes along each dimension. For example, a 2x3 matrix has a shape of (2, 3), indicating two rows and three columns. When working with tensors in AI, it's crucial to ensure that tensors have compatible shapes for operations like addition, multiplication, and convolution.

Tensor operations are at the heart of neural network computations. These operations include element-wise operations, matrix multiplication, convolution, and more.

Element-wise operations are applied to corresponding elements of tensors of the same shape, making them a fundamental building block for various neural network layers and operations.

Matrix multiplication is a crucial operation for linear transformations in neural networks. It is used in fully connected layers to compute weighted sums of input data and weight matrices. Matrix multiplication enables neural networks to model complex relationships between inputs and outputs.

Convolution is a specialized operation used in convolutional neural networks (CNNs) for processing grid-like data, such as images. Convolutional layers apply filters (kernels) to input data, sliding them across the input grid and computing local weighted sums. Convolutional operations help capture spatial patterns and hierarchical features in images.

Tensor reshaping is another essential operation for rearranging data within tensors. It allows you to change the shape of a tensor while preserving the total number of elements. Reshaping operations are used for flattening data, preparing inputs for neural network layers, and converting between different tensor shapes.

Broadcasting is a concept in tensor operations that enables you to perform operations on tensors with different shapes in a compatible manner. Broadcasting automatically expands the dimensions of smaller tensors to match the shape of larger tensors, facilitating element-wise operations.

Reduction operations aggregate information within tensors. Common reduction operations include summing along specific axes, finding the maximum or minimum values, and calculating means or variances. Reduction operations are used for pooling and computing statistics in neural networks.

Activation functions are non-linear operations applied to tensors within neural network layers. Activation functions introduce non-linearity into the model, allowing neural networks to learn complex mappings from inputs to outputs. Common activation functions include sigmoid, tanh, and ReLU.

Normalization operations standardize input data by scaling and shifting it to have a specific mean and variance. Normalization techniques, such as batch normalization and layer normalization, improve the training stability and convergence of neural networks.

Concatenation and splitting operations combine or separate tensors along specified dimensions. Concatenation is used to merge tensors, while splitting divides tensors into smaller parts. These operations are essential for building complex neural network architectures.

Transpose and permutation operations change the order of dimensions within tensors. Transposition flips the axes of a tensor, while permutation rearranges them. These operations are useful for adapting data to fit different layer requirements.

Advanced tensor operations include tensor contractions, which involve contracting multiple tensors along specific dimensions to compute more complex operations. Tensor contractions are used in tensor networks and advanced mathematical operations in AI research.

In summary, tensors and operations are fundamental concepts in neural network programming and artificial intelligence. Tensors represent data in multi-dimensional arrays, and operations allow you to manipulate and transform this data to build complex neural network architectures. Understanding these concepts is crucial for effectively designing, implementing, and training neural networks for a wide range of AI applications.

In the realm of deep learning and neural network programming, TensorFlow is a powerful framework that allows you to build and train complex machine learning models. To harness its capabilities, you'll need to understand how to construct a TensorFlow graph, which forms the foundation of your machine learning applications.

A TensorFlow graph represents a computational workflow, defining the operations and dependencies among them. Building a simple TensorFlow graph begins with importing the TensorFlow library into your Python environment, typically using the command: **import tensorflow as tf**.

Once TensorFlow is imported, you can start constructing your computational graph. The primary building block of a TensorFlow graph is the "Tensor." A tensor is a multi-dimensional array that can hold various types of data, such as numbers, images, or text.

To create a tensor, you can use the **tf.constant()** function, which allows you to specify the data you want to store in the tensor. For example, **x = tf.constant(5)** creates a tensor "x" with the value 5.

TensorFlow tensors are not evaluated immediately; they are symbolic representations of operations. To perform computations, you need to define operations within the TensorFlow graph.

Operations in TensorFlow are created using various functions provided by the library. For instance, you can use **tf.add()** to define an addition operation. To add two tensors, "a" and "b," you can create an operation like this: **c = tf.add(a, b)**.

TensorFlow operations can be visualized as nodes in a graph, where tensors flow through the edges. The graph structure defines the order of computations and dependencies between operations.

To execute operations in a TensorFlow graph, you need to create a "Session" object. The session is responsible for allocating resources and managing the execution of operations in the graph. You can create a session using the following commands:

pythonCopy code

sess = tf.Session()

Once the session is created, you can run specific operations by calling the **run()** method of the session. For example, to compute the value of the "c" tensor defined earlier, you can run: **result = sess.run(c)**.

When an operation is executed, TensorFlow automatically determines the order of computations based on the dependencies defined in the graph. It ensures that all required operations are executed before the current operation.

In addition to basic arithmetic operations, TensorFlow provides a wide range of mathematical and linear algebra functions that you can use to build complex computations. These functions include matrix multiplication, element-wise operations, and more.

TensorFlow also supports placeholder tensors, which are used for input data. Placeholders allow you to define the structure of your input data without specifying its values initially. You can later feed data into placeholders when running the session.

To create a placeholder tensor, you can use the **tf.placeholder()** function. For example, to create a placeholder for a 2D array with an unknown number of rows and three columns, you can do: **input_data = tf.placeholder(tf.float32, shape=(None, 3))**.

Placeholders are particularly useful when working with datasets because they allow you to load data dynamically during training or inference.

Variables in TensorFlow are another crucial concept. While constants have fixed values, variables can change their values as the graph is executed. Variables are often used to represent model parameters that need to be updated during training.

To create a variable in TensorFlow, you can use the **tf.Variable()** function. For instance, to create a variable "weights" initialized with zeros, you can do: **weights = tf.Variable(tf.zeros([input_dim, output_dim]))**.

Before using variables in a graph, you need to initialize them by running an operation that initializes all the variables. TensorFlow provides a convenient way to do this using the **tf.global_variables_initializer()** function.

Control flow operations, such as conditionals and loops, can also be incorporated into TensorFlow graphs. For example, you can use **tf.cond()** to define conditional statements within the graph, allowing it to adapt to different scenarios during execution.

Additionally, TensorFlow supports loops using the **tf.while_loop()** function. This enables you to create recurrent neural networks (RNNs) and implement other dynamic computations within your graph.

Once you've constructed your TensorFlow graph, it's crucial to visualize it to understand its structure and ensure it matches your intended computations. TensorBoard, a web-based tool provided by TensorFlow, allows you to visualize and debug your computational graphs effectively.

You can log important information and summaries from your graph using the **tf.summary()** functions, and then launch TensorBoard to view these visualizations. This helps you gain insights into the flow of data and dependencies within your graph.

Building a simple TensorFlow graph is just the beginning of your journey into deep learning and neural network programming. As you delve deeper into the field, you'll explore more complex operations, advanced layers, optimization techniques, and large-scale neural network architectures.

Understanding the fundamental concepts of TensorFlow graphs, tensors, operations, and sessions is essential for building and training sophisticated machine learning models, enabling you to tackle real-world AI challenges effectively.

Chapter 5: Getting Started with Keras

In the field of deep learning and neural network programming, Keras is a popular and user-friendly API that simplifies the process of building and training artificial neural networks. Keras serves as an interface to other deep learning frameworks, such as TensorFlow and Theano, making it accessible to both beginners and experienced machine learning practitioners.

One of the key advantages of Keras is its high-level API, which allows you to define neural network architectures using a simple and intuitive syntax. This abstraction hides the complexities of low-level operations, enabling you to focus on the design and experimentation of neural network models.

To get started with Keras, you'll first need to install it on your Python environment. You can do this using the **pip** package manager with the following command: **pip install keras**. Once installed, you can import Keras into your Python scripts using the **import** statement: **import keras**.

Keras provides a wide range of pre-built layers for constructing neural networks. These layers can be stacked together to create complex models. Some common types of layers include dense (fully connected), convolutional, recurrent, and normalization layers.

The Sequential model is one of the simplest ways to create a neural network in Keras. It allows you to build a neural network by adding one layer at a time in a linear fashion. To create a Sequential model, you can use the following code: **model = keras.Sequential()**.

Adding layers to the Sequential model is straightforward. You can use the **add()** method to add layers in the order you want them to appear in the network. For example, to add a dense layer with 64 units and a ReLU activation function, you can do: **model.add(keras.layers.Dense(64, activation='relu'))**.

Keras provides a wide range of activation functions that can be easily integrated into your neural network layers. Common activation functions include ReLU (Rectified Linear Unit), sigmoid, and tanh. You can specify the activation function when defining a layer.

Compiling a Keras model is the next step after defining its architecture. Compilation involves configuring the model for training by specifying loss functions, optimizers, and evaluation metrics. To compile a model, you can use the **compile()** method. For example: **model.compile(optimizer='adam', loss='categorical_crossentropy', metrics=['accuracy'])**.

Keras supports various loss functions depending on the type of problem you're solving. For classification tasks, you can use categorical cross-entropy, binary cross-entropy, or other custom loss functions. For regression tasks, mean squared error is a common choice.

Optimizers in Keras are responsible for updating the model's weights during training to minimize the loss function. Popular optimizers include Adam, RMSprop, and Stochastic Gradient Descent (SGD). You can choose the optimizer that best suits your problem and model.

Before training a Keras model, you need to prepare your data by preprocessing it. Data preprocessing may include normalizing input values, splitting data into training and validation sets, and one-hot encoding categorical variables.

Keras provides convenient tools for data preprocessing, such as the **keras.preprocessing** module. For example, you can use **keras.preprocessing.image.ImageDataGenerator** to perform real-time data augmentation for image datasets.

Training a Keras model involves feeding it with training data, updating weights during each iteration (epoch), and evaluating its performance on a validation set. You can use the **fit()** method to train a model. For instance: **model.fit(x_train, y_train, epochs=10, batch_size=32, validation_data=(x_val, y_val))**.

Batch size is a hyperparameter that determines the number of samples used in each forward and backward pass during training. Choosing an appropriate batch size can impact the training speed and model generalization.

Validation data is essential for monitoring the model's performance during training and preventing overfitting. Keras allows you to specify a validation dataset when training, and it provides callbacks like early stopping to halt training when the model's performance on the validation set stops improving.

Callbacks in Keras are useful for performing actions during training, such as saving model checkpoints, adjusting learning rates, and visualizing training progress. You can create custom callbacks or use built-in ones like **ModelCheckpoint** and **ReduceLROnPlateau**.

Keras supports various ways to visualize training progress. You can use the **History** object returned by the **fit()** method to plot training and validation loss and accuracy over epochs. Additionally, tools like TensorBoard integration provide more in-depth visualizations.

Once a Keras model is trained, you can evaluate its performance on a test dataset using the **evaluate()** method. This allows you to obtain metrics such as accuracy, loss, and other specified evaluation metrics.

In addition to the Sequential model, Keras also supports the Functional API, which provides greater flexibility for creating complex neural network architectures with multiple inputs and outputs. The Functional API is ideal for building models like Siamese networks, multi-modal networks, and models with shared layers.

Transfer learning is a powerful technique in deep learning, and Keras simplifies the process of leveraging pre-trained models. You can load pre-trained models like VGG16, ResNet, or Inception, remove or fine-tune certain layers, and use them as feature extractors or starting points for your own models.

Keras offers an extensive library of pre-processing layers and utilities for handling various types of data, including text, images, and sequences. These tools facilitate data preparation and feature extraction when working with real-world datasets.

Keras is highly extensible, allowing you to create custom layers, loss functions, and callbacks to tailor the framework to your specific needs. This flexibility makes it suitable for a wide range of applications beyond standard deep learning tasks.

In summary, Keras provides a user-friendly and versatile API for building and training neural networks. Its high-level interface simplifies the development process, making it accessible to both beginners and experts in deep learning. By understanding the core concepts and workflows of Keras, you can efficiently create and train neural networks for various machine learning and artificial intelligence applications.

Creating your first Keras model is an exciting step on your journey into the world of deep learning and artificial neural networks. To start, you'll need to import the Keras library into your Python environment, which can be done using the **import** statement: **import keras**.
Keras offers a simple and intuitive interface for building neural network models, making it accessible to both beginners and experienced machine learning practitioners. One of the primary components of a Keras model is the "Sequential" container, which allows you to define a neural network as a sequence of layers. You can create a Sequential model using the **Sequential()** constructor: **model = keras.Sequential()**.
Once you have created a Sequential model, you can start adding layers to it. In Keras, layers are building blocks that process data as it flows through the network. The first layer you add to a Sequential model should specify the input shape, which defines the shape of the data that the model will receive. For example, if you are working with image data with dimensions 28x28 pixels and three color channels (RGB), you can define the input shape as follows: **model.add(keras.layers.Input(shape=(28, 28, 3)))**.
After specifying the input shape, you can add various types of layers to your model. Common types of layers include dense (fully connected) layers, convolutional layers, and recurrent layers. Each layer type is suited to different types of data and tasks. For example, dense

layers are often used in feedforward neural networks for tasks like image classification, while convolutional layers are essential for image processing and computer vision tasks.

To add a dense layer to your model, you can use the **Dense()** function. This function allows you to specify the number of units (neurons) in the layer and the activation function to be applied to the layer's output. For instance, to add a dense layer with 128 units and a ReLU activation function, you can do: **model.add(keras.layers.Dense(128, activation='relu'))**.

In addition to specifying the number of units and activation function, you can further customize the behavior of each layer by adding additional arguments. These arguments include kernel initializers, bias initializers, and regularizers. These options allow you to fine-tune the performance and behavior of your neural network.

Adding more layers to your model allows you to create deeper and more complex neural networks. You can experiment with different layer types, sizes, and activations to design a model that is suitable for your specific task. It's important to note that the order in which you add layers to the model determines the flow of data through the network. Layers added later in the sequence receive the output from the preceding layers as input.

After you have defined the architecture of your model by adding layers, you need to compile it before training. Compilation involves specifying essential details like the loss function, optimizer, and evaluation metrics. The loss function measures the error between the model's predictions and the actual target values. Common loss functions include mean squared error for regression tasks and categorical cross-entropy for classification tasks.

To compile your model, you can use the **compile()** method, specifying the loss function, optimizer, and evaluation metrics as arguments. For example: **model.compile(loss='mean_squared_error', optimizer='adam', metrics=['accuracy'])**.

The optimizer is responsible for updating the model's weights during training to minimize the loss function. Popular optimizers include Adam, RMSprop, and stochastic gradient descent (SGD). The choice of optimizer depends on the specific task and the characteristics of your dataset.

Evaluation metrics are used to assess the performance of the model during training and evaluation. Common evaluation metrics for classification tasks include accuracy, precision, recall, and F1 score. For regression tasks, metrics like mean absolute error (MAE) and root mean squared error (RMSE) are often used.

Once your model is compiled, you can start training it on your dataset. Training a neural network involves feeding it with input data and target values, iteratively updating the model's weights to minimize the loss function. You can use the **fit()** method to train your model, passing the input data and targets as arguments. For example: **model.fit(X_train, y_train, epochs=10, batch_size=32, validation_data=(X_val, y_val))**.

The **fit()** method allows you to specify the number of training epochs, batch size, and validation data. Epochs represent the number of times the entire dataset is passed forward and backward through the network during training. Batch size determines the number of samples processed in each forward and backward pass. Validation data is used to monitor the model's performance on a separate dataset during training, helping you identify overfitting and track progress.

During training, the model's weights are updated using an optimization algorithm specified during compilation. The optimization algorithm adjusts the weights in a way that minimizes the loss function. As the number of epochs increases, the model gradually improves its ability to make predictions on the training data.

Validation data helps you assess how well the model generalizes to unseen data. By monitoring the performance on the validation dataset, you can make informed decisions about when to stop training or adjust hyperparameters. This prevents the model from becoming too specialized to the training data and ensures that it performs well on new, unseen examples.

In addition to training and evaluation, Keras provides tools for model prediction and inference. Once your model is trained, you can use it to make predictions on new data by calling the **predict()** method. For example: **predictions = model.predict(X_test)**.

The **predict()** method returns the model's predictions for the input data, allowing you to use the trained neural network for tasks like classification, regression, and more. You can also interpret the model's output and make decisions based on its predictions.

Keras supports a wide range of customization options, allowing you to fine-tune your model and experiment with different architectures. You can explore advanced topics like regularization, dropout, and batch normalization to improve model performance and generalization.

In summary, creating your first Keras model is an essential step in mastering deep learning and neural network programming. Keras simplifies the process of building and training neural networks, making it accessible to both beginners and experts in the field. Understanding the core concepts of defining model architecture, compiling, training, and evaluating models is essential for tackling a wide range of machine learning and artificial intelligence tasks. As you gain more experience, you can explore advanced techniques and architectures to build more sophisticated models and address complex real-world challenges.

Chapter 6: Building Your First Neural Network

Designing the architecture of a neural network is a critical step in creating effective machine learning models. The architecture defines the structure of the network, including the number of layers, the types of layers, and the connections between them. The architecture you choose should be tailored to the specific problem you're solving, as different tasks require different network designs.

One of the first decisions to make when designing a neural network architecture is determining the type of neural network to use. For example, if you're working on an image classification task, you might consider using a Convolutional Neural Network (CNN), which is designed to process grid-like data such as images.

On the other hand, if you're dealing with sequential data like text or time series, a Recurrent Neural Network (RNN) or its variants like Long Short-Term Memory (LSTM) networks might be more suitable. Each network type has its strengths and weaknesses, so understanding the nature of your data and problem is crucial.

Once you've chosen the type of neural network, you need to decide on the overall architecture. This involves determining the number of layers and their sizes. For deep learning tasks, you may opt for networks with many layers (deep networks), while shallow networks may suffice for simpler tasks.

Deep networks can capture complex hierarchical features but require more data and computation. Shallow networks, on the other hand, are computationally efficient but may struggle with tasks that involve learning intricate patterns. The balance between depth and computational resources depends on your problem's complexity and the available data.

When designing the architecture, consider the input and output layers. The input layer should match the dimensionality of your input data. For example, if you're working with grayscale images of size 28x28 pixels, your input layer should have 784 neurons (28 * 28). If your data is more complex, you might need to perform preprocessing or feature extraction before feeding it into the network.

The output layer's design depends on the task. For binary classification problems, a single neuron with a sigmoid activation function is often sufficient. For multi-class classification, you might use a softmax activation function with as many neurons as there are classes. Regression tasks typically have a single neuron in the output layer.

The layers between the input and output layers are called hidden layers. The choice of the number of hidden layers and their sizes is a crucial design decision. A common architecture for feedforward neural networks involves using densely connected (fully connected) layers. The number of neurons in each hidden layer, also known as the width of the layer, can vary.

Selecting the right number of neurons in the hidden layers requires some experimentation and understanding of your data. Too few neurons may result in underfitting, where the network fails to capture complex patterns. Too many neurons may lead to overfitting, where the network memorizes the training data but doesn't generalize well to new data.

Regularization techniques, such as dropout and L1/L2 regularization, can help mitigate overfitting. They introduce constraints on the network's weights, making it more robust to noise and preventing it from fitting the training data too closely.

Activation functions play a crucial role in neural network architectures. Common activation functions include ReLU (Rectified Linear Unit), sigmoid, and tanh. ReLU is a popular choice for hidden layers due to its simplicity and effectiveness. However, for the output layer, the choice of activation function depends on the task.

For binary classification, a sigmoid activation function is suitable, as it squashes the output to a value between 0 and 1. For multi-class classification, a softmax activation function is used to obtain probabilities for each class. Regression tasks typically use linear activation functions for the output layer to predict continuous values.

Designing the architecture also involves deciding how layers are connected. In feedforward neural networks, each neuron in a layer is connected to every neuron in the next layer. This full connectivity allows the network to capture complex relationships.

In some cases, you may want to introduce skip connections or shortcuts between layers. Skip connections, often used in deep neural networks like ResNet, help combat the vanishing gradient problem and enable the network to learn more effectively.

When designing the architecture, consider the computational resources available. Deeper networks with more neurons require more memory and processing power. If you have limited resources, you may need to design a smaller network or explore techniques like transfer learning.

The choice of loss function is another critical design decision. The loss function quantifies the error between the model's predictions and the actual target values. The choice of loss function depends on the task.

For regression tasks, mean squared error (MSE) is a common choice. It measures the average squared difference between predicted and actual values. For classification tasks, cross-entropy-based loss functions like binary cross-entropy and categorical cross-entropy are widely used. They assess the dissimilarity between predicted class probabilities and true class labels.

Selecting the right optimizer is essential for training the network efficiently. Popular optimizers include Adam, RMSprop, and stochastic gradient descent (SGD). Each optimizer has its advantages and may perform differently depending on the problem.

Learning rate is a hyperparameter that controls the step size during optimization. Choosing an appropriate learning rate is crucial, as too high a learning rate may lead to divergence, while too low a learning rate may result in slow convergence.

It's common practice to monitor the training process using validation data. Validation data allows you to assess the model's performance on data it hasn't seen during training. This helps you detect overfitting and determine when to stop training.

Early stopping is a technique where training is halted when the model's performance on the validation set starts to degrade. It prevents the model from overfitting the training data.

Designing the architecture of a neural network is a creative process that involves experimentation and iterative refinement. You may need to try different configurations, hyperparameters, and architectures to find the best solution for your problem.

Implementing the forward and backward pass in a neural network is a fundamental aspect of training deep learning models. The forward pass involves taking input data, passing it through the network's layers, and generating predictions. The backward pass, also known as backpropagation, is the process of computing gradients with respect to the loss function and updating the model's parameters to minimize the loss.

To implement the forward pass, you start by feeding your input data into the input layer of the neural network. The input data should be properly preprocessed and transformed to match the network's input dimensions.

As the input data flows through the network, it undergoes a series of transformations, with each layer applying a set of weights and biases to the input. These weights and biases are the parameters of the network that need to be learned during training.

Each layer computes an intermediate representation of the data based on its weights, biases, and activation function. The intermediate representations are also known as activations. The activations from the previous layer serve as input to the next layer in the network.

The forward pass continues layer by layer until the data reaches the output layer, where it produces predictions for the given input. The output layer's activation function depends on the nature of the problem you're solving. For example, for binary classification, a sigmoid activation function may be used, while softmax is common for multi-class classification.

During the forward pass, the network calculates a loss value that quantifies the error between its predictions and the actual target values. The choice of loss function depends on the type of task, such as mean squared error for regression or cross-entropy for classification.

The forward pass essentially computes the predicted output of the neural network based on the current values of its weights and biases. However, these values are initially random and do not produce accurate predictions.

The goal of the backward pass is to update the network's parameters (weights and biases) to minimize the loss and improve prediction accuracy. This process involves computing gradients of the loss with respect to the network's parameters using the chain rule of calculus.

The key concept behind backpropagation is the gradient descent algorithm, which is used to update the parameters. Gradient descent adjusts the weights and biases in the direction that minimizes the loss. The magnitude of the adjustment is controlled by a hyperparameter called the learning rate.

The first step in the backward pass is to compute the gradient of the loss with respect to the output of the network. This gradient represents how much the loss would change for a small change in the network's output. For example, if the network predicted a value of 0.7 for a binary classification problem, and the true target value is 1, the gradient of the loss with respect to the output would be -0.3.

Once the gradient with respect to the output is known, it is propagated backward through the network using the chain rule. Each layer in the network computes the gradient of its activations with respect to its inputs and the gradient of its inputs with respect to its parameters.

The gradients are calculated layer by layer, starting from the output layer and moving backward towards the input layer. At each layer, the gradients from the previous layer are used to compute the gradients for that layer. These gradients indicate how much the loss would change with respect to changes in the layer's weights and biases.

Backpropagation calculates these gradients efficiently by reusing intermediate results from the forward pass. This process is computationally efficient and allows deep neural networks to be trained effectively.

Once the gradients are computed for all layers, the network's parameters are updated using gradient descent. The new parameter values are determined by subtracting the gradients multiplied by the learning rate from the current parameter values. This process nudges the parameters in the direction that reduces the loss.

It's essential to adjust the learning rate carefully, as too large a learning rate may cause the optimization process to diverge, while too small a learning rate may result in slow convergence. Learning rate scheduling techniques can help adapt the learning rate during training to balance these issues.

Backpropagation and gradient descent are iterative processes. Training continues for multiple epochs, with each epoch consisting of a forward pass, a backward pass, and parameter updates. Over time, the network's parameters converge to values that minimize the loss function and produce accurate predictions.

During training, it's crucial to monitor the loss on both the training data and a separate validation dataset. This allows you to track the network's performance and detect issues like overfitting. Early stopping is a technique where training is halted if the validation loss starts increasing, indicating that the model is overfitting.

Additionally, regularization techniques like dropout and L1/L2 regularization can help prevent overfitting by introducing constraints on the network's parameters.

Implementing the forward and backward pass in a neural network requires careful attention to detail and a solid understanding of the mathematical principles behind the process. Frameworks like TensorFlow and PyTorch simplify the implementation of these operations, allowing you to focus on designing and experimenting with different network architectures and hyperparameters.

In summary, the forward pass involves passing input data through the network to make predictions, while the backward pass (backpropagation) computes gradients to update the network's parameters and minimize the loss. This iterative process, combined with gradient descent, is the foundation of training neural networks and allows them to learn complex patterns from data.

Chapter 7: Training and Fine-Tuning Models

Gradient descent is a fundamental optimization algorithm used in training machine learning and deep learning models. It plays a crucial role in finding the values of model parameters that minimize a given loss function.

The primary objective of training a machine learning model is to find the best set of model parameters that can make accurate predictions. To achieve this, we need an optimization algorithm that can iteratively adjust the parameters in a way that minimizes the error or loss between predicted and actual values.

Gradient descent is such an optimization algorithm that relies on the gradient of the loss function with respect to the model parameters. The gradient represents the direction of the steepest ascent in the loss landscape, and gradient descent moves in the opposite direction to minimize the loss.

The core idea behind gradient descent is to start with an initial guess for the parameters and iteratively update them. At each iteration, the gradient of the loss function is computed with respect to the current parameter values.

The gradient provides information on how much each parameter should be adjusted to reduce the loss. Parameters that contribute more to the loss receive larger updates, while parameters that have less impact receive smaller updates.

The learning rate is a hyperparameter that determines the step size taken during each iteration of gradient descent. Choosing an appropriate learning rate is crucial because a too-small learning rate can result in slow convergence, while a too-large learning rate may cause the optimization process to diverge.

There are different variants of gradient descent, each with its characteristics and methods for determining the learning rate. One common variant is the stochastic gradient descent (SGD), which randomly selects a subset of the training data, called a mini-batch, to compute the gradient.

SGD is computationally efficient and often converges faster than the batch gradient descent, which computes the gradient using the entire training dataset. Another variant is the mini-batch gradient descent, which falls between SGD and batch gradient descent in terms of computational cost and convergence speed.

One important aspect of gradient descent is the choice of loss function. The loss function quantifies the difference between the model's predictions and the actual target values. The gradient of the loss function is computed to determine how much each parameter should be updated.

Common loss functions include mean squared error (MSE) for regression tasks and categorical cross-entropy for classification tasks. The choice of loss function depends on the nature of the problem you're trying to solve.

Gradient descent has several variations and extensions to address challenges that may arise during optimization. One such extension is momentum, which introduces a moving average of the past gradients to smooth the parameter updates and accelerate convergence.

Another extension is the adaptive learning rate, which adjusts the learning rate during training to speed up convergence and avoid divergence. Popular adaptive learning rate algorithms include AdaGrad, RMSprop, and Adam.

When using gradient descent in practice, it's essential to monitor the training process by tracking the loss on both the training and validation datasets. This helps detect issues like overfitting and ensures that the model generalizes well to unseen data.

Early stopping is a technique used to halt training when the validation loss starts increasing, indicating that the model is overfitting the training data. Regularization techniques like L1 and L2 regularization can also help prevent overfitting by adding penalties to the loss based on the magnitude of the parameters.

Gradient descent is a versatile and widely used optimization algorithm that forms the foundation of training machine learning and deep learning models. It allows models to learn from data and adapt their parameters to make accurate predictions.

Despite its effectiveness, gradient descent can sometimes get stuck in local minima or saddle points in the loss landscape. This issue has led to the development of advanced optimization techniques, such as second-order optimization methods and stochastic variants like SAGA and Adam.

The choice of optimization algorithm depends on various factors, including the problem's complexity, the amount of available data, and the computational resources at hand. In practice, it's common to experiment with different optimization algorithms and hyperparameters to find the most effective combination for a specific task.

In summary, gradient descent is a fundamental optimization algorithm used in machine learning and deep learning to update model parameters iteratively. It relies on the gradient of the loss function to determine how parameters should be adjusted to minimize the loss. Various variants and extensions of gradient descent exist to address different challenges and improve convergence speed. Choosing the right optimization algorithm and hyperparameters is an essential part of training machine learning models and achieving optimal performance.

Hyperparameter tuning and regularization are crucial aspects of training machine learning and deep learning models to achieve optimal performance. Hyperparameters are parameters that are not learned from the data but are set before training, such as the learning rate and batch size. Regularization techniques are used to prevent overfitting, where a model performs well on the training data but poorly on unseen data.

Hyperparameter tuning involves the process of finding the best combination of hyperparameters that lead to the highest model performance. It is often an iterative and time-consuming task that requires experimenting with different hyperparameter values and evaluating their impact on the model's performance.

One common approach to hyperparameter tuning is grid search, where a predefined set of hyperparameters is systematically explored by training and evaluating the model for each combination. Another approach is random search, where hyperparameters are randomly sampled from predefined distributions.

More advanced techniques like Bayesian optimization and genetic algorithms can also be used for hyperparameter tuning, as they can efficiently search the hyperparameter space to find optimal values.

The choice of hyperparameters can significantly affect a model's training and generalization performance. For example, the learning rate determines the step size during optimization and can impact convergence and the quality of the learned parameters. A learning rate that is too high may cause divergence, while one that is too low may lead to slow convergence.

Batch size, which determines the number of training samples used in each iteration, can influence both training speed and model generalization. Larger batch sizes may lead to faster training but can result in less generalization, while smaller batch sizes may slow down training but lead to better generalization.

The number of hidden layers and neurons in a neural network is another critical hyperparameter that affects the model's capacity and ability to fit the training data. Deeper networks with more neurons can capture complex patterns but may be prone to overfitting if not properly regularized.

Regularization techniques are used to mitigate overfitting by adding constraints or penalties to the model during training. One common regularization method is L1 regularization, which adds a penalty based on the absolute values of the model's parameters. L2 regularization, on the other hand, adds a penalty based on the square of the parameters.

These regularization techniques encourage the model to have smaller and more sparse parameter values, reducing its capacity to fit noise in the training data. Regularization is often controlled by a hyperparameter called the regularization strength, which determines the trade-off between fitting the training data and preventing overfitting.

Dropout is another popular regularization technique that randomly drops a fraction of neurons during each training iteration. This helps prevent co-adaptation among neurons and encourages the network to learn more robust features. The dropout rate is a hyperparameter that determines the probability of dropping neurons in each layer. Early stopping is a form of regularization that halts training when the model's performance on the validation dataset starts degrading. It prevents the model from continuing to fit the training data too closely and overfitting.

Data augmentation is a technique used in computer vision tasks to increase the effective size of the training dataset. It involves applying random transformations to the training data, such as rotations, translations, and flips. Data augmentation can help the model generalize better by exposing it to a more diverse set of training examples.

Hyperparameter tuning and regularization often go hand in hand, as finding the best hyperparameters can also help prevent overfitting. Regularization techniques can be adjusted and tuned as hyperparameters to find the right balance between fitting the training data and generalizing to unseen data.

Cross-validation is a valuable technique for evaluating hyperparameter choices and assessing the model's generalization performance. It involves splitting the training data into multiple folds and training the model on different subsets while validating on the remaining fold. Cross-validation provides a more robust estimate of the model's performance and helps avoid overfitting to a single validation split.

Hyperparameter tuning and regularization require a combination of domain knowledge, experimentation, and computational resources. It is common to use automated hyperparameter tuning libraries like scikit-learn's GridSearchCV or TensorFlow's Keras Tuner to streamline the process.

In deep learning, the architecture itself, including the number of layers and their sizes, is often considered a hyperparameter that can be tuned. Architectural choices, such as the use of convolutional layers, recurrent layers, or attention mechanisms, can significantly impact a model's performance.

Hyperparameter tuning and regularization are ongoing processes that may need to be revisited as new data becomes available or as the problem evolves. Regularization techniques should be carefully chosen and adjusted based on the characteristics of the data and the model's behavior during training.

In summary, hyperparameter tuning and regularization are critical for training machine learning and deep learning models that generalize well to unseen data. Finding the right combination of hyperparameters and regularization techniques requires experimentation and a deep understanding of the problem and the model. By carefully tuning hyperparameters and applying appropriate regularization, you can build models that achieve high performance and robustness in various machine learning tasks.

Chapter 8: Handling Data for Neural Networks

Data preprocessing and cleaning are essential steps in the data science pipeline that significantly impact the quality and reliability of the models and insights derived from data analysis. Raw data, collected from various sources, is often messy, incomplete, and inconsistent, making it necessary to preprocess and clean the data before it can be used effectively.

The first step in data preprocessing is data collection, where data is gathered from different sources, such as databases, APIs, files, or sensors. During this stage, it is crucial to ensure that data is collected in a structured and organized manner to facilitate subsequent processing.

Data cleaning involves identifying and rectifying errors and inconsistencies in the data. Common data cleaning tasks include handling missing values, correcting typos, and dealing with duplicate records. Missing values can be problematic as they may lead to biased analysis or modeling results.

One common approach to handling missing values is imputation, where missing data is replaced with estimated values. Imputation methods can be as simple as replacing missing values with the mean or median of the feature, or they can be more advanced, such as using regression models to predict missing values.

Duplicate records in the data can arise due to various reasons, such as data entry errors or system glitches. Identifying and removing duplicate records is essential to prevent skewing the analysis or modeling results.

Data cleaning also involves addressing outliers, which are data points that deviate significantly from the majority of the data. Outliers can negatively impact statistical analyses and machine learning models. Common techniques for handling outliers include data transformation, trimming, or removing extreme values.

Inconsistent data formats, such as inconsistent date formats or units of measurement, should also be addressed during data cleaning. Standardizing data formats ensures that all data points are in a consistent and usable format.

Data preprocessing also includes feature engineering, which involves creating new features or modifying existing ones to improve the performance of machine learning models. Feature engineering aims to extract meaningful information from the data and represent it in a way that is more suitable for modeling.

For example, in natural language processing, text data can be transformed into numerical features using techniques like TF-IDF or word embeddings. In image analysis, features can be extracted from images using methods like edge detection or feature detectors.

Scaling and normalization are common preprocessing techniques used to standardize the range of numerical features. Scaling ensures that all numerical features have the same scale, preventing certain features from dominating others during modeling.

Normalization, on the other hand, transforms features to have a standard normal distribution with a mean of zero and a standard deviation of one. These techniques are particularly important for algorithms that rely on distance-based metrics, such as K-means clustering or support vector machines.

Categorical data, which consists of discrete values like colors or categories, often needs to be encoded into numerical form for machine learning models to process. One-hot encoding is a common technique for converting categorical data into a binary vector representation.

Data preprocessing may also involve handling imbalanced datasets, where one class significantly outnumbers the others. In such cases, techniques like oversampling or undersampling can be applied to balance the dataset and prevent model bias.

Data preprocessing is not a one-time task but an iterative process. As new data is collected or the problem evolves, the preprocessing steps may need to be adjusted or expanded. It's important to maintain flexibility in the preprocessing pipeline to accommodate changing data requirements.

Another crucial aspect of data preprocessing is data exploration and visualization, which helps identify patterns, trends, and relationships within the data. Exploratory data analysis (EDA) involves generating summary statistics, creating data visualizations, and performing statistical tests to gain insights into the data's characteristics.

Visualization techniques, such as scatter plots, histograms, and heatmaps, can reveal patterns, correlations, and anomalies in the data. EDA can also help in feature selection by identifying which features are most relevant to the problem at hand.

Data preprocessing and cleaning are essential for ensuring that the data used for analysis or modeling is accurate, reliable, and representative of the underlying problem. Inadequate data preprocessing can lead to biased or inaccurate results, affecting the quality of insights and models.

It's important to document and maintain a record of the preprocessing steps applied to the data. This documentation helps ensure transparency and reproducibility of the data preprocessing pipeline, making it easier for others to understand and replicate the process.

The choice of data preprocessing techniques depends on the specific characteristics of the data and the goals of the analysis or modeling. It is essential to tailor the preprocessing steps to the unique challenges and requirements of each dataset and problem.

Data preprocessing is often an iterative and exploratory process that requires domain knowledge and a deep understanding of the data's context. Effective data preprocessing can lead to more accurate models, improved insights, and better decision-making in various fields, including healthcare, finance, marketing, and more.

In summary, data preprocessing and cleaning are essential steps in the data science pipeline, ensuring that raw data is transformed into a clean, structured, and informative format. These steps involve handling missing values, correcting errors, dealing with outliers, and preparing the data for analysis or modeling. Effective data preprocessing can significantly impact the quality and reliability of data-driven solutions and insights.

Data augmentation techniques are a crucial component of the data preprocessing pipeline, especially in the realm of computer vision and natural language processing. These techniques aim to increase the diversity and size of the training dataset by applying various transformations to the existing data.

One of the primary motivations behind data augmentation is to improve the generalization capability of machine learning models. By exposing the model to a more extensive range of data variations, it becomes more robust and better equipped to handle real-world scenarios.

In computer vision tasks, data augmentation techniques are particularly prevalent. One common transformation is image rotation, where the image is rotated by a certain degree. This helps the model learn to recognize objects or patterns from different orientations.

Another widely used technique is image flipping, which horizontally mirrors the image. This is especially valuable for tasks where the orientation of the object doesn't matter, such as image classification.

Image cropping involves taking a random section of the image, which can help the model learn to focus on specific features or objects within the image.

To simulate changes in lighting conditions, image brightness and contrast can be adjusted. This variation helps the model become more invariant to different lighting scenarios.

Zooming in and out of images by resizing them is another effective data augmentation technique. This allows the model to recognize objects or patterns at different scales.

In natural language processing, data augmentation techniques are used to create variations in text data. One common method is text augmentation through synonym replacement. In this technique, certain words in a sentence are replaced with synonyms, maintaining the overall context but introducing variations.

Text paraphrasing involves rephrasing sentences while preserving their original meaning. This helps the model learn to understand similar sentences with different phrasing.

For audio data, data augmentation can involve changing the pitch, speed, or adding background noise. These transformations help the model become more robust to variations in audio input.

Data augmentation is not limited to a single transformation; multiple transformations can be applied simultaneously. For example, in image classification, an image can be rotated, flipped, and cropped in combination.

A critical consideration when applying data augmentation is ensuring that the augmented data remains representative of the underlying distribution. If the augmentations introduce unrealistic variations, the model may become confused or perform poorly.

Data augmentation can be particularly valuable when the training dataset is limited or imbalanced. By generating additional training examples, the model can better capture the underlying patterns in the data.

While data augmentation is a powerful technique, it's essential to use it judiciously and consider the specific requirements of the task. Excessive or inappropriate augmentation can lead to overfitting, where the model becomes too specialized on the augmented data and doesn't generalize well.

Moreover, data augmentation should be applied only to the training dataset, not the validation or test sets. The goal is to simulate a more diverse training dataset while keeping the evaluation dataset representative of the real-world scenarios the model will encounter.

In some cases, domain-specific data augmentation techniques are developed to address specific challenges. For example, in medical imaging, specialized augmentations may be used to simulate different imaging conditions or diseases.

Data augmentation can also be part of a larger data preprocessing pipeline that includes other techniques like normalization, feature extraction, and data scaling.

Deep learning frameworks and libraries often provide built-in support for data augmentation. These libraries offer easy-to-use functions and parameters for specifying the desired augmentations.

In computer vision, libraries like TensorFlow and PyTorch include image augmentation modules that allow users to apply various transformations to images.

In natural language processing, data augmentation libraries offer functionalities like text augmentation, making it easier to generate variations of text data.

While data augmentation can significantly improve the performance of machine learning models, it should be combined with other best practices in model development. This includes proper data splitting, model selection, hyperparameter tuning, and evaluation on independent test sets.

In summary, data augmentation techniques are a critical tool in the data scientist's toolkit, enhancing the diversity and size of training datasets. These techniques are particularly valuable in computer vision and natural language processing tasks, where they help models generalize better to real-world scenarios. However, data augmentation should be applied judiciously and in combination with other model development best practices for optimal results.

Chapter 9: Common Challenges and Troubleshooting

Overfitting and underfitting are common challenges in machine learning that impact the ability of models to generalize from training data to unseen data. They represent opposite ends of a spectrum in terms of model performance and have distinct characteristics and solutions.

Overfitting occurs when a machine learning model learns the training data too well, capturing noise and random fluctuations in addition to the underlying patterns. As a result, the model performs exceptionally well on the training data but poorly on new, unseen data.

Overfit models have high complexity, often with too many parameters or features relative to the amount of training data available. These models effectively memorize the training data, rather than learning to generalize from it.

One way to detect overfitting is by observing a significant gap between the model's performance on the training data and its performance on the validation or test data. If the model's accuracy is much higher on the training data than on new data, it is a sign of overfitting.

Overfitting can be mitigated through various techniques, with the most common being regularization. Regularization introduces constraints on the model's complexity, typically by adding a penalty term to the loss function based on the magnitude of model parameters.

L1 regularization (Lasso) encourages sparse model parameters by adding a penalty proportional to the absolute values of the parameters. This encourages the model to select only the most important features and discard less relevant ones.

L2 regularization (Ridge) adds a penalty proportional to the square of the parameters' values, promoting smaller parameter values and reducing the impact of outliers.

Another regularization technique is dropout, primarily used in neural networks. Dropout randomly deactivates a fraction of neurons during each training iteration, preventing co-adaptation among neurons and improving model robustness.

Early stopping is a simple but effective technique for mitigating overfitting. It involves monitoring the model's performance on a validation dataset during training and stopping when the validation loss starts to increase, indicating overfitting.

Increasing the amount of training data is one of the most powerful ways to combat overfitting. With more data, the model has a better chance of learning the underlying patterns rather than memorizing noise.

Underfitting, on the other hand, occurs when a model is too simple to capture the underlying patterns in the training data. Underfit models have high bias and low variance, leading to poor performance on both the training data and unseen data.

Underfitting can be recognized when the model's performance on both the training and validation data is subpar, and there is no significant performance gap between them.

To address underfitting, it is essential to increase the model's complexity. This can involve using more complex algorithms, increasing the number of features, or using a more sophisticated model architecture.

Ensemble methods, such as random forests or gradient boosting, are effective at reducing underfitting by combining multiple weak models to create a stronger one. Feature engineering plays a crucial role in addressing underfitting by providing the model with more informative features. Feature selection techniques can help identify the most relevant features to include in the model.

Hyperparameter tuning is another way to combat underfitting. By optimizing hyperparameters like the learning rate, the number of layers, or the depth of a decision tree, the model can be fine-tuned to better fit the data.

Understanding the bias-variance trade-off is key to managing overfitting and underfitting. Bias refers to the error introduced by approximating a real problem, which may be complex, by a simplified model. Variance, on the other hand, is the error introduced by the model's sensitivity to small fluctuations in the training data.

Balancing bias and variance is essential to achieve a model with good generalization performance. Too much bias leads to underfitting, while too much variance leads to overfitting.

The bias-variance trade-off is often visualized as a U-shaped curve. At the left end of the curve, where the model is too simple, bias is high, and variance is low, resulting in underfitting. At the right end of the curve, where the model is too complex, variance is high, and bias is low, leading to overfitting.

The goal is to find the sweet spot in the middle of the curve, where both bias and variance are balanced, resulting in a model that generalizes well to new data.

Cross-validation is a valuable technique for evaluating a model's performance while considering overfitting and underfitting. K-fold cross-validation involves splitting the data into K subsets (folds), training the model on K-1 folds, and evaluating it on the remaining fold. This process is repeated K times, with each fold serving as the validation set once.

Cross-validation provides a more robust estimate of a model's performance and helps assess how well it generalizes to different data subsets.

Regularization, early stopping, feature engineering, and hyperparameter tuning are all essential tools in the data scientist's toolkit for managing overfitting and underfitting.

The choice between these techniques depends on the specific problem, the available data, and the characteristics of the model. In practice, it often involves experimentation and iteration to find the right balance and achieve the best model performance.

In summary, overfitting and underfitting are common challenges in machine learning that impact a model's ability to generalize from training data to unseen data. Overfitting occurs when a model is too complex and learns the training data too well, while underfitting happens when a model is too simple to capture the underlying patterns. Addressing these challenges requires a combination of techniques, including regularization, feature engineering, hyperparameter tuning, and cross-validation, to strike the right balance between bias and variance and achieve optimal model performance.

Debugging neural network errors is an essential skill for

machine learning practitioners and deep learning researchers. Despite the advancements in neural network frameworks and libraries, errors and issues can still occur during model development and training.

One of the most common errors in neural networks is the infamous "vanishing gradient" problem, which occurs when the gradients during backpropagation become very small as they are propagated backward through the network layers. This often leads to slow convergence or stagnation in training.

To address the vanishing gradient problem, it is crucial to use activation functions that do not squash the gradient excessively. Rectified Linear Unit (ReLU) activations, for example, are less prone to this issue because they do not saturate for positive inputs.

Another common issue is the "exploding gradient" problem, which is the opposite of the vanishing gradient problem. In this case, gradients become extremely large during backpropagation, causing numerical instability and divergence in training.

To mitigate the exploding gradient problem, gradient clipping can be applied, which involves setting a threshold beyond which gradients are scaled down to a manageable level.

Incorrect data preprocessing can also lead to errors in neural network training. For example, if input data is not properly normalized or scaled, it can result in slow convergence or difficulty in finding the right learning rate.

Data preprocessing issues can often be resolved by ensuring that input data has a consistent and standardized format and scaling features appropriately.

Overfitting is a common error in neural network training, where the model becomes too complex and starts fitting noise in the training data. This can lead to poor generalization on unseen data.

To address overfitting, techniques like dropout, L1 and L2 regularization, and early stopping can be employed to regularize the model and prevent it from becoming overly complex.

Underfitting, on the other hand, occurs when the model is too simple to capture the underlying patterns in the data. This can result from using a model architecture with insufficient capacity or not training the model for enough epochs.

To combat underfitting, it is essential to choose an appropriate model architecture and ensure that the model has enough capacity to learn from the data. Training for a sufficient number of epochs can also help the model converge to a better solution.

Learning rate scheduling errors can cause problems during training. Choosing an inappropriate learning rate schedule can lead to slow convergence, oscillations in the loss function, or even divergence.

To optimize learning rates, it is advisable to use learning rate schedules that reduce the learning rate over time or employ adaptive learning rate algorithms like Adam or RMSprop.

Inconsistent or noisy labels in the training data can also introduce errors during neural network training. If the ground truth labels are incorrect or ambiguous, it can lead the model astray and result in suboptimal performance.

To address label-related errors, it is essential to carefully validate and preprocess the training data, ensuring that labels are accurate and consistent.

Vanishing or exploding gradients can be diagnosed by examining the gradients during training. Logging and visualizing the gradients of the model's parameters can help identify and diagnose the issue.

Regularization errors can be identified by monitoring the training and validation loss curves. If the training loss is significantly lower than the validation loss, it may indicate that the model is overfitting.

Overfitting can also be detected by examining the model's performance on a held-out validation dataset. If the validation accuracy starts to degrade while the training accuracy continues to improve, it is a sign of overfitting.

Learning rate errors can be diagnosed by plotting the learning rate schedule and observing its behavior during training. If the learning rate is too high, it can lead to rapid oscillations in the loss function or divergence.

If the learning rate is too low, the model may converge very slowly, or it may get stuck in a suboptimal solution. Monitoring the learning rate's behavior during training can help identify inappropriate learning rate schedules.

Data preprocessing errors can be identified by examining the input data statistics. Visualizing and analyzing the distribution of input features can reveal inconsistencies or scaling issues.

Overfitting can be addressed by applying appropriate regularization techniques such as dropout or weight decay. Regularization methods can help prevent the model from fitting the training data too closely and encourage it to generalize better.

Underfitting can be diagnosed by monitoring the training loss and validation loss curves. If both losses are high and don't show signs of convergence, it may indicate that the model is too simple for the task.

Addressing underfitting may require increasing the model's capacity, changing its architecture, or training it for more epochs.

Label-related errors can be detected by reviewing the training data and labels carefully. If there are inconsistencies, inaccuracies, or ambiguities in the labels, it may be necessary to clean and validate the labels.

In summary, debugging neural network errors requires a combination of diagnostic tools, careful monitoring, and domain knowledge. Common errors include vanishing and exploding gradients, data preprocessing issues, regularization problems, and label-related errors.

Detecting and resolving these errors often involves visualizing training metrics, examining gradients, and validating the data and labels. By systematically diagnosing and addressing these issues, machine learning practitioners can improve the reliability and performance of their neural network models.

Debugging neural network errors is an essential skill for machine learning practitioners and deep learning researchers. Despite the advancements in neural network frameworks and libraries, errors and issues can still occur during model development and training.

One of the most common errors in neural networks is the infamous "vanishing gradient" problem, which occurs when the gradients during backpropagation become very small as they are propagated backward through the network layers. This often leads to slow convergence or stagnation in training.

To address the vanishing gradient problem, it is crucial to use activation functions that do not squash the gradient excessively. Rectified Linear Unit (ReLU) activations, for example, are less prone to this issue because they do not saturate for positive inputs.

Another common issue is the "exploding gradient" problem, which is the opposite of the vanishing gradient problem. In this case, gradients become extremely large during backpropagation, causing numerical instability and divergence in training.

To mitigate the exploding gradient problem, gradient clipping can be applied, which involves setting a threshold beyond which gradients are scaled down to a manageable level.

Incorrect data preprocessing can also lead to errors in neural network training. For example, if input data is not properly normalized or scaled, it can result in slow convergence or difficulty in finding the right learning rate.

Data preprocessing issues can often be resolved by ensuring that input data has a consistent and standardized format and scaling features appropriately.

Overfitting is a common error in neural network training, where the model becomes too complex and starts fitting noise in the training data. This can lead to poor generalization on unseen data.

To address overfitting, techniques like dropout, L1 and L2 regularization, and early stopping can be employed to regularize the model and prevent it from becoming overly complex.

Underfitting, on the other hand, occurs when the model is too simple to capture the underlying patterns in the data. This can result from using a model architecture with insufficient capacity or not training the model for enough epochs.

To combat underfitting, it is essential to choose an appropriate model architecture and ensure that the model has enough capacity to learn from the data. Training for a sufficient number of epochs can also help the model converge to a better solution.

Learning rate scheduling errors can cause problems during training. Choosing an inappropriate learning rate schedule can lead to slow convergence, oscillations in the loss function, or even divergence.

To optimize learning rates, it is advisable to use learning rate schedules that reduce the learning rate over time or employ adaptive learning rate algorithms like Adam or RMSprop.

Inconsistent or noisy labels in the training data can also introduce errors during neural network training. If the ground truth labels are incorrect or ambiguous, it can lead the model astray and result in suboptimal performance.

To address label-related errors, it is essential to carefully validate and preprocess the training data, ensuring that labels are accurate and consistent.

Vanishing or exploding gradients can be diagnosed by examining the gradients during training. Logging and visualizing the gradients of the model's parameters can help identify and diagnose the issue.

Regularization errors can be identified by monitoring the training and validation loss curves. If the training loss is significantly lower than the validation loss, it may indicate that the model is overfitting.

Overfitting can also be detected by examining the model's performance on a held-out validation dataset. If the validation accuracy starts to degrade while the training accuracy continues to improve, it is a sign of overfitting.

Learning rate errors can be diagnosed by plotting the learning rate schedule and observing its behavior during training. If the learning rate is too high, it can lead to rapid oscillations in the loss function or divergence.

If the learning rate is too low, the model may converge very slowly, or it may get stuck in a suboptimal solution. Monitoring the learning rate's behavior during training can help identify inappropriate learning rate schedules.

Data preprocessing errors can be identified by examining the input data statistics. Visualizing and analyzing the distribution of input features can reveal inconsistencies or scaling issues.

Overfitting can be addressed by applying appropriate regularization techniques such as dropout or weight decay. Regularization methods can help prevent the model from fitting the training data too closely and encourage it to generalize better.

Underfitting can be diagnosed by monitoring the training loss and validation loss curves. If both losses are high and don't show signs of convergence, it may indicate that the model is too simple for the task.

Addressing underfitting may require increasing the model's capacity, changing its architecture, or training it for more epochs.

Label-related errors can be detected by reviewing the training data and labels carefully. If there are inconsistencies, inaccuracies, or ambiguities in the labels, it may be necessary to clean and validate the labels.

In summary, debugging neural network errors requires a combination of diagnostic tools, careful monitoring, and domain knowledge. Common errors include vanishing and exploding gradients, data preprocessing issues, regularization problems, and label-related errors.

Detecting and resolving these errors often involves visualizing training metrics, examining gradients, and validating the data and labels. By systematically diagnosing and addressing these issues, machine learning practitioners can improve the reliability and performance of their neural network models.

Chapter 10: Building a Simple AI Application

Integrating neural networks into applications is a critical step in harnessing the power of deep learning for real-world problems. Once you have trained a neural network model that performs well on your specific task, the next challenge is to deploy it effectively within an application.

The integration process involves several considerations, starting with the choice of the deployment platform. You need to decide whether your application will run on a web server, a mobile device, an edge device, or in the cloud.

Each deployment platform has its unique requirements and constraints that may impact how you integrate neural networks. For example, deploying a deep learning model on a resource-constrained edge device may require optimizing the model's size and performance.

One critical decision in deploying neural networks is choosing the right framework or library for your application. Popular deep learning frameworks like TensorFlow, PyTorch, and Keras offer deployment options and tools to help you integrate your model effectively.

Next, you need to consider the interface through which your application will interact with the neural network model. Will it be a web API, a mobile app, a command-line tool, or a desktop application?

If you opt for a web API, you'll need to create an HTTP server that exposes endpoints for receiving input data, processing it with the model, and returning predictions. Frameworks like Flask or Django can be handy for building the server.

For mobile apps, you'll need to package your model and associated code into the app and create a user-friendly interface for users to interact with the model. Mobile development frameworks like React Native, Flutter, or native development can help you achieve this.

Command-line tools and desktop applications require a different approach, with user interfaces designed for specific use cases. Python libraries like Tkinter, PyQt, or Electron for cross-platform apps can be helpful.

Scaling your application to handle multiple users or high traffic is another consideration. This may involve setting up load balancers, deploying multiple instances of your application, and optimizing resource usage to ensure smooth operation.

Security is a paramount concern when integrating neural networks into applications. You need to protect your model, data, and user information from potential threats and attacks.

Secure communication, encryption, and proper authentication mechanisms should be in place, especially if your application involves sensitive data or user privacy.

Once your application is running, it's essential to monitor its performance and the behavior of the integrated neural network model. Logging and metrics can help you track usage patterns, diagnose issues, and optimize the system over time.

Logging relevant information about input data, predictions, and errors can be invaluable for troubleshooting and improving the model's performance.

Continuous monitoring of the model's performance can help you detect drift or degradation in its accuracy.

Regularly retraining the model on updated data can mitigate these issues and ensure that it remains effective.

As your application evolves, you may need to update the integrated neural network model to reflect changing requirements or data distributions. This requires a well-defined process for model versioning, testing, and deployment.

Ensuring that model updates do not disrupt the application's functionality is crucial. A/B testing or canary deployments can be used to gradually roll out new models and assess their impact.

Optimizing the neural network model for deployment is essential for achieving efficient and responsive applications. This may involve quantization, pruning, or model compression techniques to reduce the model's size and memory footprint.

Quantization, for instance, can convert the model's parameters from 32-bit floating-point values to lower-precision data types, reducing memory and computational requirements.

Model pruning involves identifying and removing redundant or less important weights, leading to a more compact model without sacrificing performance.

Selecting the right hardware acceleration can significantly boost the performance of your integrated neural network. For example, using GPUs or TPUs can accelerate inference and reduce response times for applications.

Edge devices, such as smartphones and IoT devices, often have limited computational resources. Optimizing the neural network model for these devices is crucial to ensure smooth and responsive performance.

On-device machine learning frameworks, like TensorFlow Lite or Core ML, provide tools and optimizations for running models on edge devices efficiently.

In some cases, you may need to trade off model accuracy for efficiency, especially on resource-constrained devices. Balancing these trade-offs requires experimentation and thorough testing.

The deployment of neural networks also involves considerations around data privacy and compliance with regulations such as GDPR. You must handle user data responsibly, obtain necessary permissions, and ensure that your application complies with relevant laws and standards.

Ethical considerations are essential when integrating neural networks into applications. Bias, fairness, and transparency in model predictions should be carefully monitored and addressed to avoid unintended consequences or discrimination.

Explainable AI (XAI) techniques can help make neural network predictions more interpretable and provide insights into why certain decisions are made.

In summary, integrating neural networks into applications requires careful consideration of deployment platforms, frameworks, interfaces, scaling, security, monitoring, and optimization. Balancing performance, efficiency, and ethical considerations is essential for building robust and responsible AI-powered applications that deliver value to users while minimizing risks and unintended consequences.

Deploying your AI solution is the culmination of your efforts in developing, training, and integrating machine learning models into a practical application. It marks the transition from experimentation and research to delivering real value to users, customers, or stakeholders.

Deploying an AI solution involves several essential steps, each requiring careful planning and execution. The first step is selecting the appropriate deployment environment, which could be cloud-based, on-premises, edge devices, or a combination of these.

Cloud-based deployment offers scalability, ease of management, and access to a wide range of cloud services and infrastructure. Popular cloud providers like Amazon Web Services (AWS), Google Cloud Platform (GCP), and Microsoft Azure offer comprehensive tools and services for deploying machine learning models.

On-premises deployment may be necessary for applications with strict data privacy or regulatory requirements. In such cases, you will need to set up and maintain the necessary hardware and software infrastructure within your organization.

Edge deployment, on the other hand, involves running models on devices at the edge of the network, such as smartphones, IoT devices, or edge servers. This approach can provide low-latency and offline capabilities but requires careful optimization to run efficiently on resource-constrained devices.

Once you've chosen your deployment environment, the next step is preparing your machine learning model for deployment. This includes packaging the model, its dependencies, and any preprocessing steps into a deployable format.

Containers, such as Docker, are a popular choice for packaging machine learning models and their dependencies, ensuring consistency across different environments.

Model serving frameworks like TensorFlow Serving, PyTorch Serve, or ONNX Runtime provide tools and APIs for deploying and managing models in production.

When deploying your AI solution, it's essential to consider how you will handle model updates and versioning. Machine learning models are not static; they may require periodic updates to maintain their accuracy and relevance. Implementing a robust versioning strategy ensures that you can easily roll back to previous model versions if issues arise with new updates.

A/B testing or canary deployments can help you assess the performance of new model versions by gradually rolling them out to a subset of users while monitoring key metrics.

Scalability is a critical consideration when deploying AI solutions, especially if your application is expected to handle a large user base or a high volume of requests. Horizontal scaling, where you distribute the load across multiple instances of your application, can help you accommodate increased demand.

Load balancing solutions can help evenly distribute incoming requests across different instances of your AI application, ensuring efficient resource utilization and responsiveness.

Security is paramount in AI deployment, as machine learning models may process sensitive or confidential data. You need to implement robust security measures to protect your application and the data it handles.

Secure communication protocols, encryption, and proper authentication mechanisms should be in place to safeguard data in transit and at rest.

Regularly applying security patches and updates to your deployed models and infrastructure is crucial to address vulnerabilities and emerging threats.

Monitoring and observability are essential for maintaining the health and performance of your AI solution in production. Logging relevant information, such as input data, predictions, and errors, can help you diagnose issues and track the behavior of your application.

Implementing a centralized logging and monitoring system allows you to aggregate and analyze logs and metrics from different components of your application.

Anomaly detection and alerting mechanisms can help you identify and respond to unexpected behaviors or issues in real-time.

Performance optimization is an ongoing process in AI deployment. You should continuously monitor your application's performance, identify bottlenecks, and optimize resource utilization.

Profiling tools can help you identify areas where your application can be optimized for better efficiency and lower latency.

Efficient model inference, caching, and parallelization are common techniques for improving the performance of AI applications.

Ensuring the ethical use of AI in your deployed solution is essential. You should be aware of potential biases and fairness issues in your models and take steps to mitigate them.

Explainable AI (XAI) techniques can help make your AI system more transparent and interpretable, providing insights into why certain decisions are made.

Maintaining transparency in how AI is used and sharing information about data sources, model training, and decision-making processes can build trust with users and stakeholders.

Compliance with regulations and standards, such as GDPR in Europe or HIPAA in healthcare, is crucial when handling user data in AI applications. You must ensure that your deployment meets the legal requirements and data protection standards relevant to your domain.

Documentation and user support are often overlooked aspects of AI deployment. Providing clear and comprehensive documentation for users and developers helps them understand how to interact with your AI solution and troubleshoot issues.

User support channels, such as help desks or forums, can be instrumental in addressing user questions and resolving problems.

Continuous evaluation and improvement of your deployed AI solution are essential to ensure that it remains effective and meets evolving user needs. User feedback, monitoring data, and performance metrics can guide you in making informed decisions about updates and enhancements.

Iterative development and deployment practices, such as DevOps and continuous integration/continuous deployment (CI/CD), enable you to streamline the deployment process and respond quickly to changes and feedback.

BOOK 2
ADVANCED NEURAL NETWORK PROGRAMMING:
MASTERING DEEP LEARNING TECHNIQUES WITH
PYTHON, TENSORFLOW, AND KERAS

ROB BOTWRIGHT

Chapter 1: Deep Learning Fundamentals

Perceptrons are fundamental building blocks in artificial neural networks, serving as the foundation for more complex neural network architectures. Developed by Frank Rosenblatt in the late 1950s, perceptrons are simple binary classifiers that take input values, apply weights and a bias, and produce an output based on a threshold.

A perceptron's operation can be summarized as follows: it takes multiple input values, multiplies each input by a corresponding weight, sums up these weighted inputs, adds a bias term, and then applies a threshold function to produce the output. This threshold function is also known as the activation function.

The activation function in a perceptron typically implements a step function, where if the weighted sum of inputs and bias exceeds a certain threshold, the perceptron outputs one; otherwise, it outputs zero. This binary output makes perceptrons suitable for linearly separable problems where inputs can be classified into two categories.

While perceptrons are a crucial concept in neural network history, they have limitations. One significant limitation is that perceptrons can only solve linearly separable problems, meaning problems where a straight line can cleanly separate the two classes of data points.

For non-linearly separable problems, perceptrons cannot find a solution, making them unsuitable for many real-world tasks. To address this limitation, more advanced activation functions and neural network architectures were developed.

One key advancement in neural network design was the introduction of the sigmoid activation function, which replaced the step function used in perceptrons. The sigmoid function is a smooth, S-shaped curve that can produce continuous outputs between zero and one.

This continuous output range allows neural networks to capture and model non-linear relationships in data, making them more versatile and powerful for various tasks. The sigmoid activation function maps the weighted sum of inputs and bias to a probability-like value.

The sigmoid activation function is defined as $f(x) = 1 / (1 + e^{(-x)})$, where x is the input to the function. The steepness of the sigmoid curve around the origin is controlled by the parameter "x," and it approaches zero for large negative values of "x" and one for large positive values of "x."

One of the essential properties of the sigmoid function is that it's differentiable, which is crucial for gradient-based optimization algorithms used in training neural networks. The derivative of the sigmoid function can be expressed as $f'(x) = f(x)(1 - f(x))$, which is used in backpropagation during the training process.

The sigmoid activation function allows neural networks to model complex, non-linear relationships in data, enabling them to learn and generalize from a wide range of input patterns. However, sigmoid activations have their own limitations, particularly with the "vanishing gradient" problem.

The vanishing gradient problem occurs when gradients during backpropagation become very small as they are propagated backward through deep networks with many layers. This issue can significantly slow down or hinder the training of deep neural networks.

To mitigate the vanishing gradient problem, new activation functions were developed. One such activation function is the Rectified Linear Unit (ReLU), which has become one of the most widely used activation functions in deep learning.

The ReLU activation function is defined as $f(x) = max(0, x)$, where x is the input to the function. It produces zero for negative inputs and passes positive inputs as they are.

ReLU activations are computationally efficient and address the vanishing gradient problem by allowing gradients to flow freely for positive inputs. However, they are not without their own challenges, such as the "dying ReLU" problem, where neurons can get stuck in a state of producing zero outputs and not updating their weights during training.

To address the issues of the original ReLU, variations were introduced. One such variation is the Leaky ReLU, which allows a small gradient for negative inputs, preventing neurons from becoming inactive.

The Leaky ReLU activation function is defined as $f(x) = x$ for $x > 0$ and $f(x) = ax$ for $x <= 0$, where "a" is a small positive constant. This small gradient for negative inputs ensures that neurons with Leaky ReLU activations can recover from the "dying ReLU" problem.

Another variation is the Parametric ReLU (PReLU), which allows the slope of the activation function to be learned during training, rather than using a fixed constant as in Leaky ReLU.

The Parametric ReLU activation function is defined as $f(x) = x$ for $x > 0$ and $f(x) = ax$ for $x <= 0$, where "a" is a learnable parameter that can be updated during training.

In addition to ReLU-based activations, other activation functions like the Exponential Linear Unit (ELU) and the Swish activation have been proposed, each with its advantages and disadvantages.

The choice of activation function depends on the specific problem and the characteristics of the data. Different activation functions may be more suitable for different tasks, and experimentation is often necessary to determine the best choice.

In summary, activation functions are a crucial component of neural networks, as they determine how neurons process and transform input data. From the original step function in perceptrons to the versatile ReLU and its variations, the development of activation functions has played a significant role in the advancement of deep learning and its ability to model complex, non-linear relationships in data.

Backpropagation is a fundamental algorithm in the training of artificial neural networks, enabling them to learn from data and improve their performance. Developed in the 1970s and refined over the years, backpropagation is a cornerstone of modern machine learning and deep learning.

At its core, backpropagation is a gradient-based optimization technique that adjusts the weights and biases of neural network connections to minimize a specified loss or error function. The goal is to find the set of parameters that make the network's predictions as close as possible to the target values.

Backpropagation operates by computing the gradient of the loss function with respect to each weight and bias in the network. These gradients indicate how much each parameter should be adjusted to reduce the error.

The chain rule from calculus is a key concept underlying backpropagation. It allows us to compute gradients efficiently by decomposing the overall gradient into a sequence of smaller gradients for each layer of the network.

The process begins with a forward pass, where input data is fed through the network to compute predictions. Each layer applies a set of weights and biases to the input data, followed by an activation function that introduces non-linearity.

The activations at each layer are stored and used in the backward pass to compute gradients. During the forward pass, intermediate values and activations are cached to facilitate gradient computation.

Once predictions are made, the loss or error between the predictions and the actual target values is calculated. Common loss functions include mean squared error for regression tasks and categorical cross-entropy for classification tasks.

The goal of backpropagation is to adjust the network's parameters (weights and biases) to minimize this loss function. To achieve this, the gradient of the loss with respect to each parameter is computed.

Starting from the output layer and moving backward through the network, the gradients are computed layer by layer using the chain rule. This process gives us the gradient of the loss with respect to each parameter, indicating how the parameter should change to reduce the loss.

The gradients are used to update the parameters in the direction that decreases the loss. This update can be performed using various optimization algorithms, with stochastic gradient descent (SGD) being one of the most common choices.

SGD updates each parameter by subtracting a fraction of the gradient, known as the learning rate, from the current value. This process is repeated iteratively for a fixed number of epochs or until convergence.

Backpropagation is a computationally intensive process, especially in deep neural networks with many layers and parameters. To improve efficiency, variants of backpropagation, such as mini-batch gradient descent, are often employed.

In mini-batch gradient descent, the entire dataset is divided into smaller batches, and gradients are computed and parameter updates are performed for each batch. This approach leverages the benefits of parallelism and reduces memory requirements.

Backpropagation can be susceptible to several challenges during training, including the vanishing gradient problem and the exploding gradient problem. The vanishing gradient problem occurs when gradients become very small as they are propagated backward through deep networks with sigmoid or tanh activation functions.

Conversely, the exploding gradient problem occurs when gradients become extremely large, leading to numerical instability and divergence during training. These issues can hinder the training of deep neural networks.

To mitigate the vanishing gradient problem, activation functions like ReLU (Rectified Linear Unit) and its variants have become popular choices. These activation functions do not saturate for positive inputs and allow gradients to flow more freely during training.

Additionally, techniques like batch normalization and skip connections have been introduced to stabilize and accelerate the training of deep networks.

Regularization techniques, such as dropout and weight decay, are often used to prevent overfitting during training. Dropout randomly sets a fraction of neuron activations to zero during each forward and backward pass, effectively introducing a form of model averaging.

Weight decay encourages the network to have smaller weights, reducing the risk of overfitting. These regularization techniques help improve the generalization performance of neural networks.

In practice, backpropagation is implemented using deep learning frameworks and libraries, which provide efficient gradient computation, parameter updates, and support for various neural network architectures. Popular frameworks like TensorFlow, PyTorch, and Keras have simplified the implementation of complex neural networks and made deep learning accessible to a wider audience.

In summary, backpropagation is a fundamental algorithm that enables neural networks to learn from data and adapt their parameters to minimize a specified loss function. By iteratively computing gradients and updating parameters, backpropagation has revolutionized machine learning and is at the core of many state-of-the-art deep learning models.

Chapter 2: Advanced TensorFlow Concepts

TensorBoard is a powerful visualization tool provided by TensorFlow that enables users to gain insights into the training process and the structure of neural networks. It offers a graphical interface to explore and analyze various aspects of machine learning experiments, making it an indispensable tool for researchers and practitioners alike.

One of the key features of TensorBoard is its ability to display real-time visualizations of training metrics during the training process. By monitoring metrics such as loss, accuracy, and learning rates, users can assess the progress of their models and make informed decisions about hyperparameters and training strategies.

TensorBoard provides interactive charts and plots that allow users to zoom in on specific time intervals or training epochs, helping to identify trends and anomalies in the training data.

In addition to monitoring training metrics, TensorBoard offers visualization tools for understanding the architecture of neural networks. Users can view the computational graph of their models, which provides a visual representation of the network's structure and how data flows through it.

This visualization is particularly helpful for debugging and understanding complex neural network architectures. By examining the graph, users can ensure that the model is constructed as intended and check for any unexpected connections or operations.

TensorBoard also provides a feature called the Projector, which allows users to visualize high-dimensional data embeddings. This is especially useful for tasks like dimensionality reduction and visualizing the representations learned by neural networks in lower-dimensional spaces.

The Projector can display data points in 3D or 2D, making it easier to interpret and analyze. Users can interactively explore the embeddings, identify clusters, and gain insights into the quality of the learned representations.

Another valuable aspect of TensorBoard is the ability to visualize the distributions of weights and biases in neural networks. Understanding the distribution of parameters can help users identify potential issues like vanishing or exploding gradients.

TensorBoard's histogram visualization provides a clear picture of how the values of weights and biases change during training. This can aid in diagnosing problems and adjusting the network architecture or initialization techniques accordingly.

Furthermore, TensorBoard offers a profiling tool that helps users identify performance bottlenecks in their machine learning models. By analyzing the execution time of different operations, users can pinpoint areas of the code that may benefit from optimization.

The profiling tool also provides insights into GPU usage and memory consumption, helping users make efficient use of hardware resources.

TensorBoard supports distributed training scenarios, where multiple GPUs or machines are used to train deep learning models. In such cases, it can display metrics and visualizations from each device, allowing users to monitor the progress of distributed training in real time.

To use TensorBoard, users need to incorporate it into their TensorFlow code. This typically involves adding a few lines of code to log relevant data during training.

For example, users can log training metrics by creating summary operations in their TensorFlow graphs and running these operations within their training loop. These summaries are then written to a log directory, which TensorBoard can access for visualization.

To launch TensorBoard, users can use a command in their terminal, specifying the log directory. TensorBoard starts a web server and provides a URL that users can open in a web browser to access the visualization dashboard.

TensorBoard also offers a flexible plugin system that allows users to extend its capabilities with custom visualizations and dashboards. This enables users to tailor TensorBoard to their specific needs and research objectives.

Overall, TensorBoard is an indispensable tool for anyone working with TensorFlow and deep learning. It provides a rich set of visualization and profiling tools that facilitate the development, debugging, and optimization of machine learning models.

Whether you are a researcher exploring novel neural network architectures, a data scientist tuning hyperparameters for a specific task, or an engineer optimizing the efficiency of a production model, TensorBoard can help you gain valuable insights and make informed decisions throughout the machine learning lifecycle.

In summary, TensorBoard is a versatile and powerful visualization tool that enhances the development and understanding of machine learning models. With its real-time monitoring, architectural insights, data visualization, profiling, and extensibility, TensorBoard is an essential companion for researchers, data scientists, and engineers working in the field of deep learning and artificial intelligence.

Distributed TensorFlow is an advanced capability of the TensorFlow framework that allows users to scale up their machine learning workloads across multiple devices, machines, or even clusters. It addresses the need for handling large datasets, training complex models, and achieving high-performance computing in various machine learning tasks.

Machine learning models are becoming increasingly complex, and datasets are growing in size, making it essential to distribute computation and training across multiple resources. Distributed TensorFlow provides a framework for effectively utilizing distributed computing resources to accelerate the training of deep learning models.

One of the primary motivations for distributed TensorFlow is to overcome the limitations of single-machine training. Training deep neural networks on a single machine may not be feasible or efficient for large-scale tasks, as it can be slow and resource-intensive.

By distributing the training process across multiple machines, users can take advantage of parallelism to significantly reduce training times. This is crucial for industries like image recognition, natural language processing, and reinforcement learning, where large datasets and complex models are the norm.

Distributed TensorFlow follows a "data parallelism" approach, where the training dataset is divided into smaller batches, and each batch is processed independently on different devices or machines. The gradients computed during each batch's training are then aggregated and used to update the model's parameters.

To use distributed TensorFlow effectively, users need to set up a distributed computing environment. This typically involves configuring multiple machines or GPUs and setting up a communication mechanism between them.

One of the most common distributed TensorFlow configurations is the parameter server architecture. In this setup, there are multiple worker nodes responsible for computing gradients during training, and there are parameter servers that store and manage the model's parameters.

The worker nodes fetch the current model parameters from the parameter servers, compute gradients during training, and send these gradients back to the parameter servers for aggregation and updating the model. This distributed setup allows for efficient parameter updates and synchronization.

Distributed TensorFlow can be used with various communication frameworks, such as TensorFlow's built-in gRPC-based communication or other specialized solutions like Horovod or TensorFlow's tf.distribute library. These communication mechanisms facilitate data exchange between nodes and ensure efficient coordination in the distributed environment.

Scaling out machine learning workloads using distributed TensorFlow offers several advantages. First, it allows users to train larger models that can capture more complex relationships in data. This is essential for achieving state-of-the-art performance in tasks like image classification, natural language understanding, and recommendation systems.

Second, distributed TensorFlow enables users to process larger datasets efficiently. In industries like healthcare and finance, where datasets can be massive, distributed training is necessary to analyze and learn from the available data effectively.

Third, distributed training can lead to faster convergence of models. When multiple devices or machines are working on different parts of the dataset simultaneously, the model parameters can be updated more frequently, potentially reducing the time required to achieve a desirable level of performance.

Furthermore, distributed TensorFlow enhances fault tolerance. If one machine or GPU fails during training, the distributed setup can continue running on the remaining resources, minimizing disruptions and ensuring that valuable training progress is not lost.

However, distributed TensorFlow also introduces challenges that need to be addressed. One challenge is managing the complexity of the distributed environment, including configuring and maintaining multiple machines or GPUs. This requires expertise in distributed systems and infrastructure management.

Another challenge is ensuring efficient data distribution and synchronization. Efficient data shuffling and distribution strategies are crucial to prevent bottlenecks and maximize resource utilization.

Additionally, users must carefully tune hyperparameters, such as the learning rate and batch size, to ensure optimal convergence in a distributed setting. Poorly chosen hyperparameters can lead to slow convergence or training instability.

Monitoring and debugging distributed TensorFlow jobs can be more challenging than single-machine setups. Tools like TensorBoard can help users visualize training progress and diagnose issues, but understanding the interactions between multiple nodes can still be complex.

In summary, distributed TensorFlow is a powerful framework for scaling up machine learning workloads and tackling large-scale and computationally intensive tasks. By leveraging multiple devices, machines, or clusters, users can train complex models, process massive datasets, and achieve high-performance computing for a wide range of machine learning applications.

However, adopting distributed TensorFlow requires careful planning, infrastructure setup, and parameter tuning. Users should be prepared to address the challenges of managing a distributed environment and optimizing their training pipelines to fully harness the benefits of distributed computing in machine learning.

Chapter 3: Customizing Keras Models

Building custom layers is a powerful feature in deep learning frameworks like TensorFlow and PyTorch, allowing users to extend neural network architectures beyond the built-in layers. Custom layers enable the implementation of novel operations, complex transformations, and specialized components tailored to specific tasks.

To build custom layers, users typically need a deep understanding of the framework's API and its computational graph. Custom layers are often created by subclassing existing layer classes provided by the framework, and this process involves defining the layer's forward pass, backward pass, and other necessary methods.

One common reason for building custom layers is to implement a novel activation function. While deep learning frameworks come with a variety of built-in activation functions like ReLU and sigmoid, researchers and practitioners may develop new activation functions for specific use cases.

Custom activation functions can be defined as layers that apply a non-linear transformation to their inputs during the forward pass. These functions introduce non-linearity into the neural network, allowing it to model complex relationships in data.

Implementing a custom activation function typically involves defining its forward pass, which computes the output given the input, and the backward pass, which computes gradients during backpropagation. These gradients are crucial for updating the model's weights and biases during training.

Custom layers can also be used to implement operations that don't have a direct equivalent in the built-in layers. For example, in computer vision tasks, users may want to create a custom layer for spatial transformations like affine transformations or grid warping.

By building a custom layer, users can define the transformation's parameters, compute the transformed output during the forward pass, and calculate the gradients for backpropagation during the backward pass.

Another common use case for custom layers is designing attention mechanisms in neural networks. Attention mechanisms have proven to be effective in natural language processing and other sequence-based tasks, and they involve complex computations that require custom layers for implementation.

Building a custom attention layer involves defining how the attention scores are computed between input elements and how the weighted sum of inputs is calculated based on these scores. The layer must also compute gradients during backpropagation to train the model effectively.

In addition to novel activation functions and attention mechanisms, custom layers can be used to implement specialized regularization techniques. For example, dropout and batch normalization are widely used regularization techniques, but users may want to experiment with new regularization methods tailored to their specific datasets and tasks.

Creating a custom regularization layer involves defining the additional loss terms and gradients that need to be added during training. This allows users to integrate custom regularization techniques seamlessly into their neural network architectures.

Moreover, custom layers can be used to build neural network components that are not readily available in standard layer libraries. For instance, in reinforcement learning, users may want to create custom layers for policy networks or value networks that require specialized architectures.

By building custom layers, users have full control over the network's design, allowing them to experiment with different architectures and components to find the most suitable solution for their tasks.

When building custom layers, it's essential to consider efficiency and performance. Custom layers should be implemented in a way that leverages the framework's optimization capabilities, such as GPU acceleration and automatic differentiation.

Efficient implementation ensures that custom layers can be seamlessly integrated into existing neural network architectures, and that training and inference remain computationally tractable.

To ensure numerical stability and gradient correctness, custom layers must be rigorously tested and validated. This includes verifying that the gradients computed during the backward pass are correct and that the layer behaves as expected in various scenarios.

Deep learning frameworks like TensorFlow and PyTorch provide extensive documentation and resources for building custom layers, including tutorials, examples, and best practices. Users can refer to these resources to learn how to create and integrate custom layers effectively.

Additionally, the deep learning community often shares custom layer implementations and code snippets on platforms like GitHub and research publications. Studying existing implementations can be valuable for learning how to build custom layers and understanding their practical applications.

In summary, building custom layers is a crucial skill for deep learning practitioners and researchers. Custom layers enable the extension of neural network architectures, the implementation of novel operations, and the development of specialized components tailored to specific tasks.

Whether it's creating custom activation functions, attention mechanisms, regularization techniques, or unique network components, custom layers provide the flexibility and control needed to advance the state of the art in deep learning.

By mastering the creation of custom layers and adhering to best practices, users can push the boundaries of what is achievable with deep neural networks and develop innovative solutions to complex machine learning challenges.

Custom loss functions play a crucial role in training neural networks for various machine learning tasks. While deep learning frameworks provide a wide range of built-in loss functions, there are cases where users need to create custom loss functions tailored to their specific objectives or datasets.

To implement custom loss functions, users need to understand the mathematical formulation of the loss they want to optimize and how to integrate it into the training process. Custom loss functions are often employed in tasks like image segmentation, object detection, and generative modeling, where standard loss functions may not capture the desired behavior.

One common scenario for implementing custom loss functions is when dealing with imbalanced datasets. In many real-world applications, the distribution of classes or outcomes may be highly skewed, making it challenging for standard loss functions to handle.

For example, in medical image analysis, detecting rare diseases may lead to imbalanced datasets where the majority of samples belong to the negative class. To address this issue, users may want to design a custom loss function that assigns different weights to different classes, penalizing the misclassification of the minority class more severely.

Custom loss functions allow users to define the loss computation based on the specific characteristics of their problem. In the case of class imbalance, a custom loss function can incorporate class weights to give more importance to the minority class, helping the model focus on correctly identifying rare cases.

Another common use case for custom loss functions is when dealing with structured data or sequential data. For instance, in natural language processing tasks like machine translation, the loss function may need to account for the sequential nature of the data.

To address this, users can create a custom loss function that considers the alignment between source and target sequences and incorporates additional factors, such as sequence length or the probability of generating a correct word.

Building custom loss functions involves defining the mathematical expression that quantifies the discrepancy between the model's predictions and the ground truth. This expression often depends on the specific task and the desired behavior of the model.

For regression tasks, where the goal is to predict continuous values, users may design custom loss functions based on metrics like mean squared error or Huber loss. These loss functions can be adapted to incorporate additional terms or regularization based on the task's requirements.

For classification tasks, where the goal is to assign samples to discrete classes, custom loss functions can take various forms. Users may create loss functions that consider class imbalance, multi-class scenarios, or hierarchical classification structures.

In cases where the loss function involves complex computations or non-standard operations, users can leverage automatic differentiation provided by deep learning frameworks to compute gradients efficiently. This ensures that the gradients needed for backpropagation are computed correctly and efficiently during training.

When implementing custom loss functions, it's crucial to consider not only the forward pass, which computes the loss, but also the backward pass, which computes gradients. Gradients are essential for updating the model's parameters during training.

Deep learning frameworks like TensorFlow and PyTorch offer tools and APIs for creating custom loss functions and incorporating them into the training process. Users can define loss functions as callable Python functions or classes that inherit from predefined loss classes in the framework.

For example, in TensorFlow, users can define a custom loss function as a Python function that takes the true labels and predicted values as input and returns the computed loss. This function can be passed as an argument to the training loop or optimizer.

In PyTorch, custom loss functions can be implemented as Python classes that inherit from the **nn.Module** base class. These classes define the forward pass for loss computation and can be easily integrated into PyTorch models.

Once custom loss functions are defined, they can be used just like built-in loss functions in the training process. Users need to compute the loss using the custom loss function during each forward pass, and the framework will automatically compute gradients during backpropagation.

Testing and validation are essential when implementing custom loss functions. Users should thoroughly evaluate the effectiveness of their custom loss functions on validation datasets and monitor how they impact model performance during training.

Users may also want to consider using regularization techniques in combination with custom loss functions to prevent overfitting and improve generalization.

In summary, custom loss functions are a valuable tool for customizing machine learning models to specific tasks and datasets. They allow users to define the loss computation based on the problem's characteristics and objectives, whether it involves class imbalance, structured data, or other complexities.

By implementing custom loss functions effectively, users can fine-tune their models, achieve better performance on challenging tasks, and advance the state of the art in machine learning.

Chapter 4: Convolutional Neural Networks (CNNs)

Convolutional layers, often referred to as ConvNets or CNNs, are a fundamental building block in modern deep learning, particularly for tasks involving image and spatial data. These layers have revolutionized computer vision and have also found applications in fields like natural language processing and reinforcement learning.

At their core, convolutional layers are designed to automatically learn and extract meaningful features from input data. They are inspired by the human visual system, which processes visual information hierarchically by detecting simple patterns and gradually combining them to recognize complex shapes and objects.

The key operation in convolutional layers is convolution, which involves sliding a small filter, also known as a kernel, across the input data and computing the dot product between the filter and a local patch of the input. This operation is performed at every location in the input, allowing the layer to capture patterns regardless of their position.

Convolutional layers have several hyperparameters that determine their behavior. These include the size of the kernel, the number of kernels used in the layer, the stride (how much the kernel shifts at each step), and the padding (whether zeros are added around the input to maintain the spatial dimensions).

The output of a convolutional layer is called a feature map or activation map. Each feature map represents the response of a specific kernel to different local patterns in the input. By using multiple kernels, the layer can simultaneously detect various types of features.

Convolutional layers are characterized by their weight sharing and spatial hierarchy. Weight sharing means that the same set of kernel weights is applied to the entire input, which significantly reduces the number of parameters compared to fully connected layers.

Spatial hierarchy refers to the idea that lower layers capture simple features like edges and textures, while higher layers combine these simple features to represent more complex patterns and objects. This hierarchical feature extraction is a key reason for the success of convolutional neural networks.

Convolutional layers are often followed by activation functions, such as ReLU (Rectified Linear Unit), to introduce non-linearity into the network. The ReLU activation function replaces negative values with zero and helps the model learn complex, non-linear relationships in the data.

Pooling layers are another important component often used in conjunction with convolutional layers. Pooling layers reduce the spatial dimensions of the feature maps, making the network more computationally efficient and helping to abstract away minor spatial details. Max-pooling, for example, selects the maximum value within a local region of the input, effectively downsampling the feature maps.

In addition to the standard convolutional layers, there are variants like dilated convolutions, depthwise separable convolutions, and transposed convolutions, each designed for specific tasks and architectural considerations.

Dilated convolutions, for instance, introduce gaps between the elements of the kernel, allowing them to have a broader receptive field without increasing the number of parameters.

Depthwise separable convolutions split the standard convolution into depthwise and pointwise convolutions, which reduces computation and parameters while maintaining expressive power.

Transposed convolutions, also known as deconvolutions or upsampling layers, are used for increasing the spatial dimensions of feature maps, which is useful in tasks like image segmentation and image generation.

Convolutional layers have achieved remarkable success in a wide range of computer vision tasks. They have been pivotal in achieving state-of-the-art results in image classification, object detection, facial recognition, and more.

One of the breakthroughs that popularized convolutional layers was the AlexNet architecture in 2012, which significantly improved image classification performance on the ImageNet dataset. Since then, various architectures like VGG, GoogLeNet, and ResNet have further pushed the boundaries of what convolutional layers can achieve.

Transfer learning, the practice of using pre-trained convolutional networks and fine-tuning them for specific tasks, has become a standard approach in computer vision. It allows researchers and developers to leverage the knowledge learned by convolutional layers on large datasets to boost the performance of their models on smaller, task-specific datasets.

Convolutional layers are not limited to image data alone. They have been successfully applied to other domains as well. In natural language processing, for example, 1D convolutional layers can process text data efficiently and capture local patterns in sequences of words.

Furthermore, convolutional layers have found applications in reinforcement learning, where they can process raw pixel data from game environments and learn to extract relevant features for decision-making.

In recent years, attention mechanisms and transformers have gained popularity in natural language processing and have, in some cases, replaced traditional convolutional layers in certain architectures.

Despite the rise of new architectures, convolutional layers remain a critical tool in the deep learning toolbox. They continue to evolve, with ongoing research focusing on designing more efficient and expressive convolutional neural network architectures.

In summary, convolutional layers are a foundational element of deep learning, particularly in computer vision. They enable neural networks to automatically learn and extract meaningful features from input data, making them invaluable in tasks involving image and spatial information.

Convolutional layers, with their weight sharing, spatial hierarchy, and various architectural innovations, have revolutionized the field of computer vision and have found applications in a wide range of domains, including natural language processing and reinforcement learning.

Understanding the principles and capabilities of convolutional layers is essential for anyone working with deep neural networks, as they continue to play a central role in advancing the state of the art in machine learning.

Implementing convolutional neural network (CNN) architectures is a critical skill for deep learning practitioners, as these networks have proven to be highly effective in a wide range of computer vision tasks. CNNs are known for their ability to automatically learn hierarchical features from data, making them well-suited for tasks like image classification, object detection, and image segmentation.

Building CNN architectures involves designing the network's structure, specifying the number and type of layers, defining hyperparameters, and connecting the layers in a meaningful way. One of the fundamental decisions in CNN design is choosing the architecture's depth and complexity.

Shallower architectures, with fewer layers, tend to be computationally efficient and work well for simpler tasks. Deeper architectures, on the other hand, are capable of learning more complex features but require more computational resources and may be prone to overfitting, especially with limited training data.

One of the earliest and most influential CNN architectures is LeNet-5, developed by Yann LeCun and his colleagues in the 1990s. LeNet-5 consists of a series of convolutional layers followed by max-pooling layers and fully connected layers, with the final layer performing classification.

Another seminal architecture is AlexNet, which achieved a significant breakthrough in the ImageNet Large Scale Visual Recognition Challenge in 2012. AlexNet introduced a deeper and more complex architecture, with multiple convolutional and fully connected layers, as well as the innovative use of dropout for regularization.

VGGNet, developed by the Visual Geometry Group at the University of Oxford, is known for its simplicity and uniform architecture. It consists of multiple 3x3 convolutional layers stacked on top of each other, followed by max-pooling layers and fully connected layers. Google's Inception (GoogLeNet) introduced the concept of inception modules, which use multiple filter sizes within the same layer to capture features at different scales. This architecture's efficiency and ability to capture diverse features have made it a popular choice in various applications.

ResNet, short for Residual Network, addressed the challenge of training very deep networks by introducing skip connections or residual blocks. These blocks allow gradients to flow more easily during training, mitigating the vanishing gradient problem.

One of the characteristics of modern CNN architectures is the use of convolutional layers with small kernel sizes, typically 3x3 or 1x1. This design choice helps capture local and global features efficiently while reducing the number of parameters.

Implementing CNN architectures requires using deep learning frameworks like TensorFlow or PyTorch, which provide tools and abstractions for creating, training, and evaluating neural networks. Users can leverage these frameworks to build architectures from scratch or adapt existing pre-designed architectures.

To implement a CNN architecture, users need to define the network's layers, specifying the type of layers (convolutional, pooling, fully connected) and their configurations (kernel size, number of filters, activation functions, etc.). The order and connectivity of these layers are essential for the network's overall structure.

When creating CNN architectures, it's common to use activation functions like ReLU (Rectified Linear Unit) after convolutional and fully connected layers. ReLU introduces non-linearity into the network, allowing it to model complex relationships in the data.

Users also need to define the loss function, which quantifies the difference between the model's predictions and the ground truth labels. The choice of the loss function depends on the specific task, such as cross-entropy for classification or mean squared error for regression.

Training CNN architectures involves feeding batches of data through the network, computing the loss, and adjusting the network's parameters using optimization algorithms like stochastic gradient descent (SGD) or Adam. The goal is to minimize the loss by updating the weights and biases in the network.

Regularization techniques like dropout, batch normalization, and weight decay are commonly used to prevent overfitting and improve the generalization of CNN models. These techniques help the model perform well on unseen data.

Data augmentation is another critical aspect of implementing CNN architectures, especially when dealing with limited training data. Data augmentation techniques, such as random rotations, flips, and translations, create variations of the training data to expose the network to different perspectives and reduce overfitting.

One challenge in implementing CNN architectures is managing computational resources, as deeper and more complex networks require more memory and processing power. Using GPUs or TPUs can significantly accelerate training times and enable the development of larger models.

Hyperparameter tuning is also a crucial part of the implementation process, as selecting the right learning rate, batch size, and other hyperparameters can significantly impact the model's performance.

Evaluating CNN architectures involves testing them on validation datasets to monitor performance and make necessary adjustments. Users should track metrics like accuracy, precision, recall, and F1 score, depending on the specific task.

Transfer learning, the practice of using pre-trained CNN models and fine-tuning them for specific tasks, is a valuable approach when limited labeled data is available. Pre-trained models, such as those trained on ImageNet, can provide a strong starting point for various computer vision tasks.

Chapter 5: Recurrent Neural Networks (RNNs)

Sequence models are a category of machine learning models specifically designed for handling sequential data, where the order of elements matters. These models have a wide range of applications, including natural language processing, speech recognition, time series analysis, and more.

At the heart of sequence models is the ability to capture dependencies and patterns within a sequence, making them suitable for tasks like language modeling, machine translation, sentiment analysis, and named entity recognition.

One of the most basic sequence models is the Hidden Markov Model (HMM), which represents sequences as a series of hidden states connected by transitions. HMMs are used in various applications, such as speech recognition and part-of-speech tagging.

Recurrent Neural Networks (RNNs) are a powerful type of sequence model that can capture long-range dependencies within sequential data. RNNs are characterized by their recurrent connections, which allow information to flow from one time step to the next, making them suitable for tasks like language modeling and text generation.

Long Short-Term Memory (LSTM) networks are a variant of RNNs that address the vanishing gradient problem, a common issue when training deep networks. LSTMs use specialized gating mechanisms to selectively update and read information from the hidden state, making them capable of handling long sequences.

Another popular variant of RNNs is the Gated Recurrent Unit (GRU), which simplifies the architecture of LSTMs while retaining their ability to capture long-term dependencies. GRUs are computationally efficient and have been used successfully in various natural language processing tasks.

Bidirectional RNNs, or BRNNs, process sequences in both forward and backward directions, allowing them to capture dependencies from past and future time steps simultaneously. BRNNs are particularly useful when the context from both directions is relevant, such as in machine translation.

Attention mechanisms have become a central component of many state-of-the-art sequence models. These mechanisms enable the model to focus on specific parts of the input sequence when making predictions, improving performance in tasks like machine translation and text summarization.

Transformer models, introduced in the paper "Attention is All You Need" by Vaswani et al., have revolutionized sequence modeling. Transformers rely heavily on attention mechanisms and self-attention, enabling them to model long-range dependencies efficiently. They have become the backbone of many natural language processing models, including BERT, GPT, and T5.

Sequence-to-Sequence (Seq2Seq) models, which consist of an encoder and a decoder, are commonly used for tasks like machine translation and text summarization. The encoder processes the input sequence, while the decoder generates the output sequence.

Reinforcement learning can be combined with sequence models to address problems where the model interacts with an environment and receives feedback. Recurrent models can be used to represent the agent's policy, and reinforcement learning algorithms like REINFORCE can be applied for training.

Implementing sequence models requires a deep understanding of the architecture and the use of deep learning frameworks like TensorFlow or PyTorch. Users need to define the model's structure, including the type of layers, the number of hidden units, and the sequence length.

When dealing with text data, sequence models often require tokenization and embedding layers to convert words or characters into numerical representations. Embeddings can be pre-trained on large corpora or learned from scratch during training.

Training sequence models involves feeding sequences into the model, computing the loss, and updating the model's parameters using optimization algorithms like stochastic gradient descent (SGD) or Adam. Recurrent models are trained using backpropagation through time (BPTT), which involves unfolding the network over time steps.

Hyperparameter tuning is crucial when working with sequence models, as the choice of learning rate, batch size, and regularization techniques can significantly impact performance. Grid search or random search can be used to explore the hyperparameter space efficiently.

Evaluating sequence models involves using appropriate metrics for the specific task. For language modeling, perplexity is a common metric, while machine translation models may use BLEU or METEOR scores.

Understanding the limitations of sequence models is essential. RNNs, for example, struggle with capturing very long-range dependencies, and LSTMs and GRUs may have difficulty handling sequences with thousands of time steps due to memory constraints.

Addressing vanishing and exploding gradient problems, which can hinder training in deep sequence models, is an ongoing challenge. Techniques like gradient clipping and careful weight initialization can help mitigate these issues.

Incorporating external knowledge and pre-trained embeddings can enhance the performance of sequence models. For instance, pre-trained word embeddings like Word2Vec or GloVe can provide valuable context and improve the model's representations.

Ensemble methods, such as stacking multiple sequence models or combining them with other types of models, can lead to better performance and robustness.

Transfer learning, the practice of using pre-trained models and fine-tuning them for specific tasks, has become a standard approach in natural language processing. It allows researchers and developers to leverage large pre-trained models and adapt them to domain-specific tasks with limited data.

Visualizing the behavior of sequence models through techniques like attention maps can provide insights into how the model makes predictions and where it focuses its attention.

In summary, sequence models are a powerful class of machine learning models for handling sequential data. They have a wide range of applications in natural language processing, speech recognition, and other domains.

Understanding the different types of sequence models, including RNNs, LSTMs, GRUs, transformers, and Seq2Seq models, is essential for effectively applying them to various tasks.

Implementing sequence models involves designing the architecture, handling data preprocessing, training the model, and evaluating its performance.

Hyperparameter tuning, regularization techniques, and careful consideration of model limitations are critical aspects of working with sequence models.

Transfer learning, visualization, and the incorporation of external knowledge can further enhance the capabilities of sequence models.

With continuous advancements in deep learning and natural language processing, sequence models remain a vibrant and evolving field, with ongoing research and development pushing the boundaries of what is achievable with sequential data. Long Short-Term Memory (LSTM) networks are a specialized type of recurrent neural network (RNN) architecture designed to address the vanishing gradient problem associated with training deep networks. LSTMs are particularly effective for sequential data modeling, making them a cornerstone in natural language processing, speech recognition, and time series analysis.

The core innovation of LSTM networks is their ability to capture long-range dependencies in sequential data by introducing a memory cell that can store and retrieve information over multiple time steps. This memory cell allows LSTMs to remember information from earlier in the sequence and use it to make predictions or generate sequences.

LSTMs achieve this by employing several key components: the cell state, the hidden state, and three gating mechanisms. The cell state acts as the memory, while the hidden state contains information that the network deems relevant for the current prediction.

The three gating mechanisms—namely, the input gate, forget gate, and output gate—regulate the flow of information into and out of the memory cell. The input gate determines which new information should be stored in the cell state, the forget gate decides what old information should be discarded, and the output gate controls what information from the cell state should be used in the prediction.

One of the strengths of LSTMs is their ability to handle sequences of varying lengths. This property makes them suitable for tasks like speech recognition, where the duration of spoken words or phrases can vary.

In practice, LSTMs have been instrumental in achieving state-of-the-art results in a wide range of natural language processing tasks. They have been used for language modeling, machine translation, sentiment analysis, named entity recognition, and text generation.

Training LSTMs involves backpropagation through time (BPTT), where the network is unrolled over multiple time steps to compute gradients and update its parameters. While training, LSTMs learn to recognize patterns and dependencies in the input data, allowing them to make sequential predictions or generate sequences.

Regularization techniques like dropout are commonly used with LSTMs to prevent overfitting and improve generalization. Dropout randomly sets a fraction of the units in the LSTM to zero during each training step, forcing the network to become more robust.

LSTMs can be implemented using deep learning frameworks like TensorFlow and PyTorch. Users define the LSTM layers, specify the number of hidden units, and configure the input sequence length.

The choice of activation functions, such as the hyperbolic tangent (tanh) or ReLU, can influence the network's performance. LSTMs also work well with various types of input data, including text, audio, and time series data.

Understanding the architecture and hyperparameters of LSTMs is crucial for successfully applying them to various tasks. Hyperparameter tuning, including selecting the learning rate and batch size, can significantly impact training performance.

One of the challenges when working with LSTMs is managing computational resources, as training deep networks can be computationally intensive. Using GPUs or TPUs can accelerate training times and enable the development of larger models.

Evaluating LSTMs involves testing them on validation datasets to monitor performance and make necessary adjustments. Users should track metrics like accuracy, loss, and perplexity, depending on the specific task.

Transfer learning is a valuable approach when working with LSTMs, especially when limited labeled data is available. Pre-trained language models, such as GPT and BERT, can be fine-tuned for specific natural language processing tasks.

Visualizing the behavior of LSTMs can provide insights into how the network processes sequential data. Techniques like attention maps can reveal which parts of the input sequence are most relevant for making predictions.

Understanding the limitations of LSTMs is essential. While LSTMs excel at capturing long-range dependencies, they may still struggle with extremely long sequences due to memory constraints.

Addressing the vanishing gradient problem, which can hinder training in deep LSTMs, requires careful initialization and regularization techniques.

Incorporating external knowledge and pre-trained embeddings can enhance the performance of LSTMs, especially when working with text data.

Ensemble methods, such as stacking multiple LSTM models or combining them with other types of models, can lead to improved performance and robustness.

In summary, Long Short-Term Memory (LSTM) networks are a powerful class of neural networks for sequential data modeling. Their ability to capture long-range dependencies and handle sequences of varying lengths makes them essential in natural language processing, speech recognition, and time series analysis.

Understanding the architecture, hyperparameters, and regularization techniques for LSTMs is crucial for effective model development and training.

Transfer learning, visualization, and the incorporation of external knowledge are valuable strategies for enhancing the capabilities of LSTMs.

While LSTMs have made significant contributions to the field of deep learning, ongoing research and development continue to advance the state of the art in sequence modeling, opening up new possibilities for applications in various domains.

Chapter 6: Generative Adversarial Networks (GANs)

Generative Adversarial Networks (GANs) are a class of deep learning models that have revolutionized the field of generative modeling. GANs consist of two neural networks: a generator and a discriminator, trained in a competitive manner to produce high-quality, realistic data.

The generator's role is to create synthetic data samples, such as images or text, while the discriminator's job is to distinguish between real data and fake data produced by the generator. These two networks engage in a game-like scenario where they compete against each other, hence the term "adversarial."

The generator begins with random noise or an initial input and progressively refines its output to resemble real data samples. It does this by learning from the feedback provided by the discriminator.

The discriminator, on the other hand, receives both real and fake data and learns to distinguish between them. It provides feedback to the generator, essentially guiding it to produce more realistic data over time.

The training process of GANs involves several steps. First, the discriminator is trained on a dataset containing real data samples to learn to distinguish real from fake. Next, the generator is trained to produce fake data that can fool the discriminator. This back-and-forth training process continues iteratively.

The loss function used in GAN training is crucial. The generator aims to minimize the discriminator's ability to distinguish between real and fake data, while the discriminator aims to maximize its ability to make this distinction.

The loss function for the generator encourages it to produce data that is indistinguishable from real data. Common loss functions for the generator include binary cross-entropy or Wasserstein loss, depending on the GAN variant.

GANs have produced remarkable results in various domains. In image generation, for example, GANs have been used to create realistic images of faces, animals, and even artwork.

One of the most well-known GAN variants is Deep Convolutional GAN (DCGAN), which uses convolutional neural networks for both the generator and discriminator. DCGAN has been widely used in image generation tasks.

Conditional GANs, or cGANs, allow the generation process to be conditioned on specific information. For example, in conditional image generation, a cGAN can generate images of cats or dogs based on a specified label.

CycleGAN is another variant that focuses on domain-to-domain translation. It can transform images from one domain to another, such as converting photos into artistic paintings or turning horses into zebras.

Progressive Growing GANs (PGGANs) introduce a training technique that starts with lower-resolution images and gradually increases the resolution during training. PGGANs have been used to generate high-quality images with impressive detail.

Despite their success, training GANs can be challenging. They are sensitive to hyperparameters and require careful tuning. Stabilizing the training process and preventing mode collapse, where the generator produces limited diversity in output, are ongoing research areas.

GANs are not limited to image generation. They have been applied to text generation, style transfer, and even drug discovery. In text generation, for instance, GANs can generate human-like text based on a given prompt.

Understanding the architecture and training dynamics of GANs is essential for effectively using them in applications. The generator and discriminator networks need to be designed appropriately for the specific task at hand.

Regularization techniques, such as weight clipping or spectral normalization, can be applied to stabilize GAN training and improve convergence.

Evaluating the quality of GAN-generated samples often involves visual inspection or using metrics like the Inception Score or Fréchet Inception Distance (FID). These metrics assess the diversity and realism of the generated data.

Ethical considerations are important when working with GANs. Generating synthetic data that closely resembles real data can raise privacy concerns, and GANs can potentially be used to create deepfakes or manipulate content.

Research in GANs is ongoing, with new architectures and training techniques continually being developed. Efforts are also being made to mitigate biases and ethical issues associated with GAN-generated content.

In summary, Generative Adversarial Networks (GANs) are a groundbreaking class of deep learning models that have had a profound impact on generative modeling. Their competitive training process involving a generator and discriminator has enabled the creation of high-quality synthetic data in various domains.

Training GANs involves iteratively improving the generator's ability to produce realistic data while enhancing the discriminator's ability to distinguish real from fake data.

Various GAN variants, such as DCGAN, cGAN, CycleGAN, and PGGAN, have been developed for specific tasks and applications.

GANs are not without challenges, including mode collapse and training instability, but ongoing research continues to address these issues.

Understanding GAN architecture, training dynamics, and ethical considerations is essential for harnessing their potential in generating diverse and realistic data for various applications.

The field of GANs is dynamic and evolving, with continued advancements and new possibilities on the horizon.

Conditional Generative Adversarial Networks (cGANs) are a powerful extension of the GAN framework that allow for controlled and customized image generation. cGANs enable the generation of images conditioned on specific information, such as class labels or textual descriptions, making them a versatile tool for various image synthesis tasks.

In a traditional GAN, the generator produces data samples from random noise, and the discriminator's objective is to distinguish between real and fake data. cGANs introduce an additional input, typically in the form of class labels or attributes, which guides the generation process and allows for fine-grained control.

The conditional input provides a way to specify what type of data the generator should produce. For example, in the context of generating images of animals, the class label can indicate whether the desired image should be of a cat, dog, or another animal.

The generator in a cGAN takes both random noise and the conditional input as input and produces images accordingly. The discriminator, in turn, assesses the realism of the generated images while considering the provided condition.

cGANs have found widespread applications in various domains. One of the most common uses is in image-to-image translation tasks, where the goal is to convert images from one domain to another while preserving specific attributes.

For instance, a cGAN can be trained to translate black-and-white photos into color images or turn satellite images into maps. The conditional input specifies the desired transformation, allowing for precise control over the output.

Another application of cGANs is in image super-resolution, where low-resolution images are transformed into high-resolution counterparts. By conditioning the generator on the desired level of upscaling, cGANs can produce detailed and sharp images from limited-resolution inputs.

In the fashion industry, cGANs have been employed for virtual try-on applications. Users can specify the clothing item they want to try on, and the generator produces an image of a model wearing that item, providing a realistic preview of how it would look.

Text-to-image synthesis is another exciting application of cGANs. Given textual descriptions, cGANs can generate images that match the provided descriptions. For example, given a textual prompt like "a red sports car in a city," a cGAN can create an image that corresponds to that description.

Training cGANs involves providing paired data, where each sample is associated with a condition and the corresponding output. For instance, in a text-to-image synthesis task, the pairs consist of textual descriptions and the corresponding images.

The generator learns to produce images that align with the given conditions, while the discriminator's role is to assess the realism of both the real and generated samples with their respective conditions.

The loss function used in cGAN training typically combines the traditional GAN loss, which encourages the generator to produce realistic images, with an additional term that enforces alignment with the conditional input.

Architecturally, cGANs can be designed using convolutional neural networks (CNNs) for both the generator and discriminator. The conditional input is often incorporated as an additional layer or concatenated with the initial layers of the generator and discriminator networks.

In practice, cGANs require a suitable dataset that includes paired samples with associated conditions. For example, in the task of translating photos into artistic styles, the dataset would contain pairs of photos and their corresponding artistic style labels.

Evaluating the quality of cGAN-generated images can be subjective. Human judgment, as well as quantitative metrics like the Structural Similarity Index (SSI) or

Inception Score, can be used to assess the realism and alignment with the provided conditions.

cGANs also come with challenges, such as mode collapse, where the generator produces limited diversity in output, and the need for a large amount of paired data for effective training.

Addressing mode collapse often involves architectural modifications or advanced training techniques. One approach is to use a technique called "cycle consistency" in tasks like image translation to ensure that the generated image can be translated back to the original domain accurately.

In summary, Conditional Generative Adversarial Networks (cGANs) are a powerful framework for controlled and customized image generation. By providing conditional input, cGANs enable precise control over the generated output, making them suitable for a wide range of applications, including image translation, super-resolution, virtual try-on, and text-to-image synthesis.

Training cGANs involves using paired data with associated conditions, and architectural choices include using CNNs for both the generator and discriminator.

Evaluating cGAN-generated images can be subjective and often relies on human judgment and quantitative metrics.

Despite challenges like mode collapse and the need for sufficient paired data, cGANs continue to advance the field of image generation and hold promise for future applications in image synthesis and manipulation.

Chapter 7: Transfer Learning and Fine-Tuning

Leveraging pretrained models is a powerful technique in the field of machine learning and deep learning. These models, often called pretrained neural networks or pretrained embeddings, are models that have been trained on large datasets for specific tasks, such as image classification, natural language processing, or speech recognition.

The idea behind pretrained models is to take advantage of the knowledge captured by these models and apply it to new tasks or domains. This approach can significantly reduce the amount of data and computation required to achieve high performance on a new task.

In computer vision, pretrained models like Convolutional Neural Networks (CNNs) trained on ImageNet have become a standard starting point for various image-related tasks. These models have learned to recognize a wide range of features and patterns in images, making them useful for tasks like object detection, image segmentation, and image generation.

In natural language processing, pretrained models have had a transformative impact on tasks such as text classification, sentiment analysis, and machine translation. Models like BERT (Bidirectional Encoder Representations from Transformers) have learned contextual word representations, allowing them to capture the meaning of words in context.

One of the advantages of pretrained models is that they can be fine-tuned on specific tasks with relatively small amounts of task-specific data. This fine-tuning process adapts the pretrained model's knowledge to the new task, making it highly effective.

For example, in natural language processing, a pretrained model like BERT can be fine-tuned on a sentiment analysis dataset to create a sentiment classification model. Similarly, in computer vision, a pretrained CNN can be fine-tuned for a custom object recognition task.

The availability of pretrained models and their open-source implementations, often provided by research and industry organizations, has democratized access to state-of-the-art techniques. Researchers and practitioners can start with a pretrained model as a foundation and build upon it for their specific applications.

When using pretrained models, it's essential to understand the architecture of the model and the domain it was pretrained on. This knowledge helps in selecting the right pretrained model for a given task and making informed decisions during fine-tuning.

In some cases, transfer learning can be applied by using pretrained models in a feature extraction capacity. For instance, in image analysis, the features extracted by layers in a pretrained CNN can be used as input features for another machine learning model, such as a support vector machine or a decision tree.

Ensemble techniques, which combine multiple models' predictions, can also benefit from pretrained models as base models. By combining the predictions of multiple pretrained models, ensemble models can achieve even higher performance.

One of the key considerations when leveraging pretrained models is the amount of task-specific data available. The more data you have for fine-tuning, the better the pretrained model can adapt to the new task.

Data augmentation techniques can be used to artificially increase the size of the training dataset, which is particularly helpful when data is limited. For example, in image classification, data augmentation can include random rotations, flips, and scaling of images.

Regularization techniques, such as dropout or weight decay, may also be applied during fine-tuning to prevent overfitting, especially when the task-specific dataset is small.

Ethical considerations are essential when using pretrained models, especially in applications like natural language processing, where models may inadvertently capture biases present in the training data. Bias mitigation strategies and fairness assessments should be part of the model development process.

Evaluating the performance of a pretrained model on a new task often involves using appropriate evaluation metrics specific to the task. For example, in image classification, accuracy or F1 score may be used, while in natural language processing, metrics like precision, recall, and F1 score are common.

Visualizations and interpretability techniques can help gain insights into the pretrained model's behavior and understand why it makes certain predictions. Attention maps, saliency maps, and feature visualizations can provide valuable insights.

In summary, leveraging pretrained models is a valuable strategy in machine learning and deep learning. These models capture knowledge from large datasets and can be fine-tuned for specific tasks, making them accessible and effective for various applications.

Understanding the architecture and domain of pretrained models is crucial for selecting the right model and fine-tuning effectively.

Data augmentation, regularization, and ethical considerations play important roles in the successful use of pretrained models.

Evaluating pretrained models on new tasks involves appropriate metrics and interpretability techniques to gain insights into model behavior.

As the field of machine learning continues to advance, pretrained models will likely play an increasingly significant role in accelerating the development of intelligent systems across various domains.

Fine-tuning is a critical technique in machine learning and deep learning that allows pretrained models to be adapted to specific tasks or domains. It builds upon the knowledge captured by pretrained models and tailors it to a new, task-specific context, resulting in models that are both efficient and effective for the desired application.

The idea behind fine-tuning is to leverage the representations learned by a pretrained model and modify them to suit the target task. Pretrained models are typically trained on massive datasets for tasks such as image classification, natural language understanding, or speech recognition.

These models acquire a wide range of knowledge about features, patterns, and relationships in the data. Fine-tuning takes advantage of this knowledge and adapts it for a narrower, domain-specific goal.

In computer vision, fine-tuning pretrained Convolutional Neural Networks (CNNs) is a common practice. For example, a pretrained CNN that has learned to recognize various objects in images can be fine-tuned for a specific object detection or classification task.

The process of fine-tuning usually involves three main steps. First, the pretrained model's layers are frozen, meaning their weights are kept fixed. This preserves the general knowledge captured by the model.

Second, additional layers are added on top of the pretrained model. These layers are specific to the target task and are randomly initialized or initialized using task-specific data if available.

The third step is to train the entire model on the task-specific dataset. During training, the gradients from the task-specific loss function are propagated back through the added layers and, if allowed, into the frozen layers of the pretrained model. This fine-tuning process adapts the model to the target task.

Fine-tuning offers several advantages. One of the key benefits is the reduction in training time and data requirements. Since the pretrained model has already learned useful representations, fine-tuning typically converges faster and requires less task-specific data compared to training a model from scratch.

Moreover, fine-tuning often results in models that generalize well. The pretrained model has learned valuable features from diverse data sources, making it robust and transferable to new tasks.

Fine-tuning is widely used in natural language processing (NLP). Models like BERT, GPT, and RoBERTa have achieved state-of-the-art results by learning contextual word representations on vast text corpora. These pretrained language models can be fine-tuned for a wide range of NLP tasks, including text classification, sentiment analysis, and named entity recognition.

In the context of reinforcement learning, fine-tuning is also a valuable technique. Reinforcement learning models, such as deep reinforcement learning agents, can be pretrained using simulated environments or tasks and then fine-tuned in a real-world environment. This approach accelerates the learning process and improves the model's performance in the target environment.

Choosing the right architecture for fine-tuning is crucial. The pretrained model should have architecture and representations that are suitable for the target task. For example, a pretrained CNN designed for image classification may not be the best choice for a segmentation task.

The depth and complexity of the added task-specific layers depend on the complexity of the target task. For simpler tasks, a few additional layers may suffice, while more complex tasks may require deeper and more intricate architectures.

Hyperparameter tuning, including learning rates and batch sizes, is essential during the fine-tuning process. Optimal hyperparameters may differ from those used during the initial pretraining phase, so experimentation is necessary.

Regularization techniques, such as dropout or weight decay, are important for preventing overfitting during fine-tuning. Regularization helps ensure that the model generalizes well to unseen data.

In some cases, domain-specific data augmentation techniques may be applied during fine-tuning to increase the model's robustness. For example, in image classification, data augmentation can include random rotations, translations, or scaling of images.

Monitoring and evaluating the fine-tuning process is crucial. Tracking metrics such as accuracy, loss, or task-specific performance metrics helps assess the model's progress and determine when it has reached satisfactory performance.

Validation datasets are essential for fine-tuning, allowing the model to generalize to unseen examples. Cross-validation or split validation can help ensure the model's reliability.

Fine-tuning pretrained models requires careful consideration of ethical and fairness issues. The pretrained model may inherit biases present in the training data, which can lead to biased predictions on task-specific data.

To mitigate bias and ensure fairness, it's important to assess and address potential biases in the pretrained model's representations. Ethical considerations should be part of the fine-tuning process.

In summary, fine-tuning is a valuable technique in machine learning and deep learning that leverages pretrained models to adapt to specific tasks. It combines the knowledge captured by pretrained models with task-specific adaptations, resulting in efficient and effective models.

Fine-tuning is widely used in computer vision, natural language processing, reinforcement learning, and other domains. Choosing the right architecture, hyperparameters, regularization techniques, and monitoring strategies are essential for successful fine-tuning.

Ethical considerations, fairness assessments, and bias mitigation should be integral parts of the fine-tuning process to ensure responsible and unbiased model deployment.

Chapter 8: Natural Language Processing (NLP) with Neural Networks

Word embeddings are a fundamental concept in natural language processing (NLP) that enable computers to understand and represent words in a numerical format. These numerical representations capture semantic relationships between words, allowing machines to perform various NLP tasks, such as text classification, sentiment analysis, and machine translation.

One of the most popular word embedding techniques is Word2Vec, short for "Word to Vector." Word2Vec was introduced by researchers at Google in 2013 and has since become a cornerstone of NLP.

The primary idea behind Word2Vec is to learn dense vector representations, also known as embeddings, for words in a large corpus of text. These embeddings are designed to capture the context and meaning of words based on their usage in the text.

In Word2Vec, each word in a vocabulary is associated with a unique vector in a high-dimensional space. The dimensionality of these vectors is typically chosen to be in the hundreds, making them compact yet expressive.

The key intuition behind Word2Vec is the distributional hypothesis, which posits that words that occur in similar contexts have similar meanings. In other words, words that are used in similar ways in a large corpus of text are likely to be related in meaning.

Word2Vec leverages this hypothesis by training a neural network to predict the context of a word based on its surrounding words. There are two main architectures for

Word2Vec: Continuous Bag of Words (CBOW) and Skip-gram.

In the CBOW architecture, the model is trained to predict a target word based on its surrounding context words. For example, given the context words "the," "quick," and "jumps," the model predicts the target word "brown" in the sentence "the quick brown jumps."

In contrast, the Skip-gram architecture reverses the task by predicting the surrounding context words based on a target word. Given the target word "brown," the model predicts the context words "the," "quick," and "jumps."

Both CBOW and Skip-gram have their strengths and weaknesses. CBOW is generally faster to train and performs well on frequent words, while Skip-gram can capture more fine-grained semantic relationships and is often preferred for rare words.

The training process in Word2Vec involves updating the word vectors using stochastic gradient descent and a negative sampling objective. Negative sampling helps the model focus on distinguishing the target word from randomly sampled negative words, making the training process more efficient.

The resulting word embeddings, once trained, can be used in a wide range of NLP tasks. One of the most common applications is word similarity or analogy tasks, where word vectors are compared to measure semantic similarity or solve analogies like "king - man + woman = queen."

Word embeddings also enable the creation of word clouds, word clouds, and semantic search engines. They provide a foundation for many downstream NLP applications, such as text classification, sentiment analysis, and named entity recognition.

Pretrained Word2Vec models are often available for multiple languages and domains, saving time and resources. These pretrained embeddings can be fine-tuned on specific tasks or used as feature vectors in machine learning models.

Evaluating the quality of word embeddings is essential. Common evaluation tasks include word similarity tasks, where the cosine similarity between word vectors is compared to human judgments, and analogy tasks, where the model's ability to solve analogies is tested.

Visualizations of word embeddings in lower-dimensional spaces, such as t-SNE plots, can provide insights into the relationships between words and help identify clusters of related words.

While Word2Vec has been influential in NLP, it is not without limitations. One limitation is that it may struggle with polysemy, where a word has multiple meanings. Word2Vec represents each word with a single vector, potentially oversimplifying the complexity of word meanings.

Additionally, Word2Vec may not capture syntactic relationships between words as effectively as semantic relationships. For example, it may not distinguish between antonyms like "good" and "bad" as well as it distinguishes synonyms.

To address these limitations, more advanced word embedding techniques have been developed, such as GloVe (Global Vectors for Word Representation) and FastText, which aim to capture both semantic and syntactic information in word embeddings.

In summary, word embeddings and Word2Vec are foundational concepts in natural language processing, enabling machines to represent words in a numerical format. Word2Vec leverages the distributional hypothesis and neural networks to learn dense vector representations for words, capturing their semantic relationships.

Word embeddings have a wide range of applications in NLP tasks and provide a basis for many downstream applications. Pretrained embeddings, evaluation metrics, and visualizations are valuable tools for working with word embeddings.

While Word2Vec has been influential, it is important to consider its limitations and explore more advanced word embedding techniques to address specific NLP challenges.

Sequence-to-sequence (Seq2Seq) models are a category of neural network architectures widely used in natural language processing (NLP) for tasks that involve input sequences being transformed into output sequences. These models have revolutionized the field of NLP by enabling the development of applications like machine translation, text summarization, and chatbots.

The fundamental idea behind Seq2Seq models is to use recurrent neural networks (RNNs) or more advanced variants, such as Long Short-Term Memory (LSTM) or Gated Recurrent Unit (GRU) cells, to process and generate sequences of data. In the context of NLP, these sequences can represent sentences, paragraphs, or even longer text passages.

One of the earliest and most well-known Seq2Seq architectures is the encoder-decoder model. This model consists of two main components: an encoder network and a decoder network.

The encoder network takes the input sequence and processes it step by step. At each step, it produces a hidden state that captures information about the input sequence up to that point. Once the entire input sequence has been processed, the encoder produces a final context vector, which is a summarized representation of the input.

The decoder network takes the context vector and generates the output sequence step by step. It uses the context vector as the initial hidden state and produces one element of the output sequence at each step. The decoder is trained to generate the correct output sequence given the input sequence.

One of the early successes of Seq2Seq models was in the field of machine translation. These models revolutionized machine translation by learning to map sentences from one language to another without the need for handcrafted rules or alignment tables.

In machine translation, the input sequence is the source language sentence, and the output sequence is the target language sentence. The Seq2Seq model effectively encodes the source sentence's meaning in the context vector and then decodes it into the target sentence.

The effectiveness of Seq2Seq models in machine translation led to their application in various other NLP tasks, such as text summarization. In text summarization, the input sequence is a longer document, and the output sequence is a shorter summary of that document.

The Seq2Seq model's ability to capture the essence of the input sequence in the context vector allows it to generate meaningful summaries by decoding the context vector into a concise representation of the document.

Chatbots and conversational agents also benefit from Seq2Seq models. In a chatbot application, the input sequence is the user's message, and the output sequence is the bot's response. The encoder processes the user's message, and the decoder generates a suitable response based on the encoded information.

Seq2Seq models can handle variable-length input and output sequences, making them versatile for many NLP tasks. However, they are not without challenges.

One challenge is the issue of vanishing gradients during training. RNN-based Seq2Seq models can struggle to capture long-range dependencies in sequences, as the gradients can diminish over time. This limitation led to the development of LSTM and GRU cells, which mitigate the vanishing gradient problem to some extent.

Another challenge is handling sequences of different lengths. In tasks like machine translation, input sentences and target sentences can vary in length. Seq2Seq models typically use techniques like padding and masking to handle sequences of different lengths effectively.

Attention mechanisms have emerged as a significant enhancement to Seq2Seq models. Attention mechanisms allow the model to focus on specific parts of the input sequence when generating each element of the output sequence. This attention mechanism improves the model's ability to capture relevant information, especially in long sequences.

Transformer-based Seq2Seq models, which rely heavily on attention mechanisms, have become the state-of-the-art in many NLP tasks. The Transformer architecture, introduced in the paper "Attention Is All You Need," has revolutionized the field by achieving remarkable performance in machine translation, text generation, and other NLP applications.

In Transformer-based Seq2Seq models, the encoder and decoder are built using self-attention layers. These layers enable the model to consider all positions in the input sequence simultaneously when computing the context vector. The use of Transformers has led to significant improvements in translation quality, allowing for more accurate and fluent translations across various language pairs. Seq2Seq models have evolved from the early encoder-decoder architectures to advanced models like Transformers. These models have transformed the landscape of NLP and opened the door to a wide range of applications, including machine translation, text summarization, and chatbots.

The challenges of vanishing gradients and handling sequences of different lengths have been addressed with techniques like LSTM and GRU cells and padding and masking.

Attention mechanisms and the Transformer architecture have further improved the capabilities of Seq2Seq models, making them the foundation of many cutting-edge NLP systems.

As NLP research continues to advance, Seq2Seq models and their variants will likely play an even more prominent role in enabling machines to understand and generate human language, leading to new and exciting applications in the field.

Chapter 9: Reinforcement Learning and Neural Networks

Reinforcement learning (RL) is a branch of machine learning that focuses on training agents to make decisions in an environment to maximize a cumulative reward. Unlike supervised learning, where models are trained on labeled data, and unsupervised learning, where models find patterns in unlabeled data, RL agents learn from interaction and experience.

In RL, an agent interacts with an environment in discrete time steps. At each time step, the agent observes the current state of the environment, takes an action based on its policy, and receives a reward from the environment. The agent's goal is to learn a policy that maximizes the expected cumulative reward over time.

The core components of an RL problem are the agent, the environment, states, actions, rewards, and the policy. The agent represents the learner or decision-maker, while the environment represents the external system with which the agent interacts. States are representations of the environment at different time steps, and actions are the choices the agent can make. Rewards are numerical values that indicate the immediate benefit or cost of taking an action in a particular state. The policy is the strategy or mapping from states to actions that the agent uses to make decisions.

The RL framework is often formalized as a Markov Decision Process (MDP), which provides a mathematical framework for modeling RL problems. An MDP consists of a set of states, a set of actions, a transition probability function, a reward function, and a discount factor.

The transition probability function defines the probability of transitioning from one state to another after taking a particular action. The reward function maps state-action pairs to immediate rewards, indicating the immediate benefit or cost of taking a specific action in a particular state.

The discount factor, often denoted as γ (gamma), represents the agent's preference for immediate rewards over future rewards. A higher discount factor makes the agent focus more on immediate rewards, while a lower discount factor makes the agent consider long-term rewards.

One of the fundamental RL algorithms is the Q-learning algorithm. Q-learning is used for finding the optimal action-value function, denoted as $Q(s, a)$, which represents the expected cumulative reward of taking action "a" in state "s" and following the optimal policy thereafter.

The Q-learning algorithm iteratively updates the Q-values based on observed rewards and transitions in the environment. Over time, the Q-values converge to the optimal values, allowing the agent to make the best decisions in each state.

Another important concept in RL is the exploration-exploitation trade-off. Exploration involves trying new actions to discover their effects and learn more about the environment. Exploitation involves choosing actions that are known to yield high rewards based on current knowledge.

Balancing exploration and exploitation is essential for effective RL. Agents can use various exploration strategies, such as ε-greedy, where they choose a random action with probability ε and the best-known action with probability 1-ε.

Policy gradient methods are a class of RL algorithms that learn the policy directly, without explicitly estimating the value function. These methods aim to find the policy that maximizes the expected cumulative reward directly.

Deep reinforcement learning (DRL) combines reinforcement learning with deep neural networks. DRL algorithms use neural networks to approximate the policy or value function, allowing agents to learn from high-dimensional sensory inputs, such as images or text.

One of the most notable DRL algorithms is Deep Q-Network (DQN), which combines Q-learning with deep neural networks. DQN has achieved impressive results in tasks like playing Atari games by learning to estimate the Q-values of actions from raw pixel inputs.

In DRL, agents often use experience replay and target networks to stabilize training. Experience replay stores past experiences (state, action, reward, next state) in a replay buffer and samples mini-batches during training. Target networks are used to stabilize the Q-value target during updates.

Policy gradient methods, such as Trust Region Policy Optimization (TRPO) and Proximal Policy Optimization (PPO), have been successful in training agents for continuous action spaces, making them suitable for tasks like robotic control and autonomous driving.

Model-based reinforcement learning is another approach where agents learn a model of the environment and plan using the model. This approach can be more sample-efficient but requires accurate modeling of the environment.

One of the significant challenges in RL is the exploration of high-dimensional and continuous action spaces. Agents must learn to make good decisions in environments with a large number of possible actions, which can be a computationally challenging task.

In addition to the exploration challenge, RL also faces issues related to sample efficiency, stability, and scalability. Training RL agents often requires a substantial amount of interaction with the environment, which can be costly and time-consuming.

Transfer learning and imitation learning are areas of RL research that aim to leverage knowledge from related tasks or human demonstrations to accelerate learning. These approaches allow agents to benefit from prior knowledge and perform better in new tasks.

Ethical considerations are essential in RL, as agents can learn undesirable behaviors or biases from training data. Ensuring that RL agents behave ethically and responsibly is a critical aspect of deploying RL systems in real-world applications.

In summary, reinforcement learning is a machine learning paradigm that focuses on training agents to make sequential decisions to maximize cumulative rewards. The core components of an RL problem include agents, environments, states, actions, rewards, and policies.

RL algorithms, such as Q-learning and policy gradient methods, are used to find optimal policies in various settings. Deep reinforcement learning combines RL with deep neural networks to handle high-dimensional input spaces. Deep Q-Networks, or DQNs, have emerged as a powerful approach in the realm of reinforcement learning (RL), particularly in the context of playing video games and solving complex control tasks. These neural network-based models have significantly advanced the field by enabling agents to learn optimal policies in high-dimensional state spaces.

DQNs combine the principles of Q-learning, a classic RL algorithm, with deep neural networks to approximate the Q-function, denoted as Q(s, a), which represents the expected cumulative reward of taking action "a" in state "s" and following the optimal policy thereafter. This fusion of Q-learning and deep learning allows DQNs to handle complex tasks with rich sensory input, such as pixel data from video games. At the core of DQNs is the Q-network, which is a deep neural network that takes the current state as input and produces Q-values for each possible action as output. The Q-values estimate the expected cumulative rewards associated with taking each action in the given state. Training a DQN involves iteratively updating the Q-network's weights to minimize the temporal difference error, also known as the TD error. The TD error represents the difference between the predicted Q-value for an action and the target Q-value.

The target Q-value is calculated using a target network, which is a copy of the Q-network that lags behind during training. By using a separate target network, DQNs stabilize the training process and prevent Q-value estimates from oscillating during updates.

One of the key innovations introduced by DQNs is experience replay. Experience replay is a memory buffer that stores past experiences, consisting of tuples (state, action, reward, next state). During training, DQNs sample mini-batches of experiences from the replay buffer to decorrelate the data and improve learning efficiency.

Experience replay not only helps break correlations in the training data but also allows DQNs to reuse experiences multiple times. This technique increases sample efficiency and helps the model learn from a broader range of experiences.

Another crucial component of DQNs is the use of epsilon-greedy exploration. Epsilon-greedy is a strategy where the agent chooses the action with the highest estimated Q-value with probability 1-ε and selects a random action with probability ε. This balance between exploitation and exploration ensures that the agent explores the environment to discover optimal policies while also exploiting known strategies.

DQNs have been notably successful in solving a wide range of challenging RL tasks. One of the landmark achievements of DQNs was demonstrated in playing Atari 2600 video games. Agents trained using DQNs were able to achieve human-level performance in many of these games by learning to interpret raw pixel data as state information and selecting actions accordingly The success of DQNs in video games highlighted their potential for applications beyond gaming. These models have been applied to control problems in robotics, autonomous vehicles, finance, and healthcare, among others.

Despite their achievements, DQNs have certain limitations. They can be sensitive to hyperparameters, requiring careful tuning to achieve stable and effective training. The choice of network architecture, learning rate, and exploration schedule can significantly impact performance.

DQNs are also known to struggle with tasks that involve partial observability or delayed rewards, as they rely on accumulating rewards over time. Addressing these challenges often requires modifications to the DQN framework, such as incorporating recurrent neural networks (RNNs) or using more advanced algorithms like Proximal Policy Optimization (PPO) or Trust Region Policy Optimization (TRPO). Furthermore, DQNs are typically limited to environments with discrete action spaces. Adapting DQNs to continuous action spaces is non-trivial and may require techniques like the use of deterministic policy gradients or actor-critic architectures. Deep Q-Networks have made significant contributions to the field of RL by demonstrating the potential of combining Q-learning with deep neural networks. Their success in handling high-dimensional state spaces and complex tasks has paved the way for further advancements in deep reinforcement learning.

The use of experience replay, target networks, and epsilon-greedy exploration has been instrumental in stabilizing the training process and improving sample efficiency.

While DQNs have achieved remarkable results in video games and various control tasks, their sensitivity to hyperparameters and limitations in handling certain RL challenges have led researchers to explore more sophisticated algorithms and architectures.

In summary, Deep Q-Networks represent a significant milestone in the development of reinforcement learning algorithms. Their ability to learn from raw sensory input and solve complex tasks has positioned them as a foundational tool in the field, with applications spanning domains beyond gaming.

Chapter 10: Practical Applications of Advanced Deep Learning

Image style transfer is a captivating application of neural networks that combines the content of one image with the artistic style of another. This technique allows you to transform your photos into unique pieces of art by mimicking the visual style of famous paintings or other artworks.

The concept of image style transfer emerged from the field of deep learning and computer vision, particularly with the use of convolutional neural networks (CNNs). CNNs are well-suited for this task because they excel at capturing hierarchical features in images, making them capable of understanding both content and style.

To achieve image style transfer, a neural network is trained to generate an image that matches the content of a given input image while incorporating the artistic style from a separate style image. The key is to define what constitutes content and style in an image and then find a way to separate and recombine these elements.

In practice, image style transfer involves three main steps: defining content, defining style, and generating the stylized image. Let's dive deeper into each of these steps.

First, defining content involves identifying the high-level objects and structures present in the content image. This typically involves the use of a pre-trained CNN, such as VGG or ResNet, to extract feature maps from the content image. These feature maps capture information about the content while discarding detailed texture and color information.

Second, defining style involves extracting the artistic features that characterize the style image. To do this, you also use a pre-trained CNN, but instead of extracting feature maps from the later layers, you focus on the activations in the earlier layers. These activations capture patterns related to textures, colors, and brushwork found in the style image.

Now that you have representations for both content and style, the next step is to generate a new image that combines these elements. This is done through an optimization process that minimizes a loss function.

The loss function consists of two components: a content loss and a style loss. The content loss measures the difference between the feature maps of the generated image and the content image. The goal is to ensure that the generated image captures the content of the original image accurately.

On the other hand, the style loss quantifies the difference in the style between the generated image and the style image. This loss encourages the generated image to adopt the textures, colors, and patterns of the style image.

To optimize the loss function and generate the final stylized image, iterative optimization techniques like gradient descent are used. The optimization process gradually modifies the generated image to minimize the content and style losses simultaneously.

One of the fascinating aspects of image style transfer is the ability to apply different artistic styles to the same content image. By using various style images, you can create a wide range of artistic variations for your photos.

The choice of content and style images is a creative decision and plays a crucial role in determining the final result. You can experiment with different combinations to achieve the desired artistic effect.

Image style transfer has practical applications beyond artistic expression. For example, it can be used to automatically apply a consistent visual style to a collection of images, making them more visually cohesive.

Moreover, it has been employed in the field of computer graphics to enhance the realism of computer-generated images by applying the styles of real-world paintings.

Image style transfer is not limited to static images; it can also be extended to videos. By applying the same style transfer techniques frame by frame, you can create dynamic, stylized videos that are visually engaging.

While image style transfer produces stunning results, it's not without its challenges. One limitation is that it requires significant computational resources, especially for high-resolution images. The optimization process can be time-consuming, and real-time style transfer for videos can be particularly demanding.

Additionally, the choice of hyperparameters and the architecture of the neural network can influence the quality of the stylized image. Finding the right balance between content and style can be a subjective task, and fine-tuning may be necessary to achieve the desired outcome.

Despite these challenges, image style transfer has become a popular and widely-used technique for creative image editing. Various software tools and libraries are available that make it more accessible to artists, photographers, and enthusiasts.

In summary, image style transfer with neural networks is a captivating application that combines the content of one image with the artistic style of another, allowing for creative transformations of photos. It involves defining content and style, generating a new image, and optimizing a loss function to achieve the desired artistic effect.

This technique has practical applications beyond art, including visual cohesion for image collections and enhancing computer-generated images. While it comes with computational challenges and subjective decision-making, it offers a powerful way to create visually striking images and videos.

Artificial Intelligence (AI) has revolutionized numerous industries, and healthcare and autonomous vehicles stand out as two fields where AI has the potential to make a profound impact.

In healthcare, AI is transforming the way medical professionals diagnose, treat, and manage patients, while in autonomous vehicles, AI is driving the development of self-driving cars and trucks.

In healthcare, AI-powered diagnostic tools are becoming increasingly common, aiding doctors in the early detection of diseases and medical conditions.

These tools can analyze medical images, such as X-rays and MRI scans, with remarkable accuracy, helping to identify abnormalities that might be missed by the human eye.

Furthermore, AI is being used to analyze vast amounts of patient data to discover patterns and insights that can inform treatment decisions.

This data-driven approach to medicine, known as precision medicine, tailors treatments to the individual characteristics of each patient, improving outcomes and reducing adverse effects.

In addition to diagnosis and treatment, AI is also being utilized for drug discovery.
Machine learning algorithms can analyze chemical compounds and predict their potential for drug development, accelerating the process of bringing new medications to market.

Telemedicine, another area benefitting from AI, enables remote consultations with healthcare professionals through video conferencing and AI-driven chatbots.
These virtual healthcare solutions improve access to medical advice and reduce the burden on healthcare facilities, especially during crises like the COVID-19 pandemic.

AI-driven wearable devices and sensors are empowering individuals to monitor their health continuously.
These devices can detect anomalies in vital signs and provide early warnings of potential health issues, enabling proactive healthcare management.

In the field of autonomous vehicles, AI plays a pivotal role in achieving safe and reliable self-driving capabilities.
Sensors, such as lidar, radar, and cameras, collect data from the vehicle's surroundings, while AI algorithms process this data to make real-time driving decisions.

Machine learning models, trained on vast datasets of driving scenarios, enable autonomous vehicles to recognize and respond to various objects, such as pedestrians, cyclists, and other vehicles, in diverse road conditions.

Furthermore, AI enhances vehicle-to-vehicle (V2V) and vehicle-to-infrastructure (V2I) communication, enabling autonomous vehicles to share information with each other and with traffic management systems.
This communication improves traffic flow, reduces congestion, and enhances safety on the road.

The development of autonomous vehicles goes beyond passenger cars.
AI-driven technologies are being applied to trucks and delivery vehicles, with the potential to transform the logistics and transportation industries.
Self-driving trucks promise increased efficiency and reduced transportation costs, making the movement of goods more economical.

AI in healthcare and autonomous vehicles, while promising, also raises important ethical and regulatory considerations.
Privacy concerns surround the collection and use of sensitive patient data in healthcare, prompting the need for robust data protection measures.

In autonomous vehicles, the safety of self-driving systems is of paramount concern.

Ensuring that AI algorithms can handle unexpected situations and make split-second decisions safely is an ongoing challenge.

Moreover, the liability framework for accidents involving autonomous vehicles is still evolving.
Determining responsibility in the event of an accident involving a self-driving car presents complex legal and ethical questions.

The development and deployment of AI in healthcare and autonomous vehicles require close collaboration between technology companies, regulatory bodies, and industry stakeholders.
Regulations and standards must be established to ensure the safe and responsible use of AI in these critical fields.

In healthcare, AI-driven solutions must be rigorously evaluated and validated to meet clinical standards.
The integration of AI into healthcare workflows should enhance the capabilities of medical professionals rather than replace them.

In autonomous vehicles, extensive testing and validation procedures are essential to ensure that self-driving systems can handle a wide range of scenarios safely.
Collaboration between automotive manufacturers, technology companies, and regulatory agencies is vital for the development of standardized safety protocols.

AI's potential to transform healthcare and autonomous vehicles is vast, but it must be harnessed responsibly and ethically.
Both fields are poised to benefit from the continued advancement of AI technologies, improving patient outcomes, and revolutionizing transportation.

In summary, AI is driving significant advancements in healthcare and autonomous vehicles.
In healthcare, AI aids in diagnosis, treatment, and drug discovery, while in autonomous vehicles, it enables self-driving capabilities with applications in passenger and commercial vehicles.

However, ethical and regulatory challenges must be addressed to ensure the safe and responsible use of AI in these critical domains.
Collaboration between industry stakeholders and regulatory bodies is essential for the successful integration of AI technologies, ultimately improving healthcare outcomes and reshaping transportation.

BOOK 3
NEURAL NETWORK PROGRAMMING
BEYOND THE BASICS: EXPLORING ADVANCED CONCEPTS
AND ARCHITECTURES FOR AI WITH PYTHON,
TENSORFLOW, AND KERAS

ROB BOTWRIGHT

Chapter 1: Deep Dive into Neural Network Architectures

Feedforward Neural Networks (FNN), often referred to as artificial neural networks or simply neural networks, are a foundational concept in the field of machine learning and artificial intelligence. These networks are designed to mimic the structure and function of the human brain, with interconnected nodes or artificial neurons that process and transform data.

At the heart of a feedforward neural network is the notion of layers, which are composed of neurons. Typically, these layers include an input layer, one or more hidden layers, and an output layer. Data is fed into the input layer, processed through the hidden layers, and generates an output from the output layer.

Each neuron in a feedforward neural network performs a weighted sum of its inputs, applies an activation function to the sum, and then passes the result to the next layer. The weights and biases associated with each connection between neurons are adjusted during training to optimize the network's performance.

One of the fundamental concepts in feedforward neural networks is the universal approximation theorem. This theorem states that a neural network with a single hidden layer containing a sufficient number of neurons can approximate any continuous function, making neural networks versatile function approximators.

The activation functions applied to neurons play a crucial role in the network's ability to model complex relationships within data. Common activation functions include the sigmoid function, hyperbolic tangent function, and rectified linear unit (ReLU) function.

The sigmoid function maps input values to a range between 0 and 1, making it suitable for binary classification problems where the network's output represents probabilities.

The hyperbolic tangent function is similar to the sigmoid but maps input values to a range between -1 and 1, offering zero-centered outputs that help with convergence during training.

The ReLU function, on the other hand, introduces non-linearity by outputting the input for positive values and zero for negative values. ReLU has become a popular choice due to its simplicity and efficiency in training deep networks.

Training a feedforward neural network involves using a supervised learning approach, where the network is presented with input data along with the corresponding target or ground truth values. The network's predictions are compared to the targets, and a loss function quantifies the error between the predictions and the actual values.

Gradient descent optimization algorithms, such as stochastic gradient descent (SGD) and Adam, are commonly used to adjust the network's weights and biases to minimize the loss function.

During the training process, the network learns to recognize patterns and relationships in the data by updating its parameters. This iterative process continues until the network converges to a state where the loss is minimized, indicating that it has learned the underlying patterns in the training data.

Overfitting, where the network performs well on the training data but poorly on new, unseen data, is a common challenge in training feedforward neural networks. To address this issue, techniques like regularization, dropout, and early stopping can be employed to prevent overfitting and improve generalization.

Feedforward neural networks are widely used in a variety of applications, including image classification, natural language processing, speech recognition, and regression tasks. They have also been applied to fields like finance, healthcare, and autonomous driving, where they excel at handling complex data and making predictions.

Convolutional Neural Networks (CNNs) are a specialized type of feedforward neural network designed specifically for image and spatial data. CNNs use convolutional layers to automatically learn hierarchical features from images, making them highly effective in tasks like image recognition and object detection.

Recurrent Neural Networks (RNNs) are another variation of feedforward neural networks that are well-suited for sequential data. RNNs have recurrent connections that allow them to maintain a hidden state and process sequences of data, making them ideal for tasks like natural language processing and time series prediction.

In recent years, deep feedforward neural networks, often referred to as deep learning, have gained immense popularity. These networks have multiple hidden layers and are capable of learning increasingly abstract and complex features from data.

The success of deep learning in various domains has been driven by advancements in hardware, the availability of large datasets, and improved training techniques. Deep neural networks have achieved remarkable results in tasks such as image classification, speech recognition, and autonomous driving.

Despite their success, deep feedforward neural networks are not without challenges. Training deep networks can be computationally intensive and requires large amounts of labeled data. Additionally, selecting the appropriate architecture, hyperparameters, and optimization techniques can be a non-trivial task.

In summary, feedforward neural networks, or artificial neural networks, form the foundation of modern machine learning and artificial intelligence. These networks consist of interconnected layers of neurons and are capable of approximating complex functions, making them versatile tools for a wide range of applications.

Their ability to automatically learn from data, recognize patterns, and make predictions has made them indispensable in fields like image recognition, natural language processing, and many others. While challenges like overfitting and hyperparameter tuning exist, the ongoing advancements in neural network research continue to drive progress in the field, pushing the boundaries of what is possible with feedforward neural networks.

Radial Basis Function Networks (RBFN) are a type of artificial neural network that differs from the more commonly known feedforward neural networks. These networks are characterized by their use of radial basis functions as activation functions, and they have applications in various fields, including function approximation, classification, and interpolation.

The concept of radial basis functions originates from mathematical interpolation, where they are used to approximate a function based on a set of known data points. In RBFNs, these functions are applied to neural networks, creating a flexible and effective model for various tasks.

One of the distinctive features of RBFNs is their architecture, which typically consists of three layers: an input layer, a hidden layer with radial basis functions, and an output layer. The input layer receives the input data, while the hidden layer processes this data using radial basis functions, and the output layer produces the network's final output.

The key to the radial basis functions' effectiveness lies in their radial symmetry and localization properties. These functions are centered around specific points in the input space and decay as the distance from these centers increases. This localization allows RBFNs to capture complex patterns in the data efficiently.

The radial basis functions in the hidden layer act as activation functions and play a crucial role in processing the input data. These functions transform the input data into a higher-dimensional space, where linear separation of classes or function approximation becomes more achievable.

The most commonly used radial basis function is the Gaussian function, which has a bell-shaped curve. The Gaussian function assigns a higher weight to inputs that are closer to the center and progressively lower weights to inputs further away. This characteristic enables RBFNs to focus on the most relevant information while ignoring distant and less influential data points.

Training an RBFN involves two primary steps: center selection and weight adjustment. In center selection, the centers of the radial basis functions are determined based on the input data. One common approach is to use a clustering algorithm, such as k-means, to identify representative points in the data.

Once the centers are selected, the weights associated with each radial basis function are adjusted during the training process. This adjustment is typically performed using techniques like gradient descent or least squares optimization to minimize the error between the network's output and the target values.

RBFNs are particularly well-suited for function approximation tasks, where the goal is to find an accurate representation of an underlying function based on a limited set of data points. Their ability to approximate complex functions with a relatively small number of centers makes them efficient for tasks like interpolation and regression.

Moreover, RBFNs have been applied to classification problems, where they can provide high accuracy and generalization. In these tasks, the output layer of the network is often designed to produce class probabilities, and the network is trained using techniques like maximum likelihood estimation or cross-entropy loss.

Another advantage of RBFNs is their ability to handle noisy data effectively. The localization property of radial basis functions helps filter out noise by assigning lower weights to outliers, making the network robust to noisy input.

However, like all neural networks, RBFNs are not without limitations. One challenge is the need to determine the appropriate number of radial basis functions and their positions. Selecting too few centers may result in underfitting, while selecting too many can lead to overfitting.

Additionally, RBFNs may not perform well on tasks with high-dimensional input data, as the curse of dimensionality can make it challenging to find suitable centers for the radial basis functions. In summary, Radial Basis Function Networks (RBFN) are a type of neural network that uses radial basis functions as activation functions in its hidden layer. These networks excel in function approximation, classification, and interpolation tasks due to the properties of radial basis functions, such as radial symmetry and localization.

Their architecture consists of an input layer, a hidden layer with radial basis functions, and an output layer. Training RBFNs involves center selection and weight adjustment, allowing them to approximate complex functions and handle noisy data efficiently.

While RBFNs have their strengths, such as accuracy and noise robustness, they also face challenges in determining the appropriate number of centers and may struggle with high-dimensional input data. Overall, RBFNs offer a unique and valuable approach to neural network modeling, with applications across various fields.

Chapter 2: Hyperparameter Optimization and Tuning

Grid Search and Random Search are two common techniques used for hyperparameter tuning in machine learning and deep learning. Hyperparameters are settings or configurations that are not learned from the data but must be specified before training a machine learning model.

Grid Search is a systematic approach to hyperparameter tuning where you define a set of possible values for each hyperparameter, and the algorithm explores all possible combinations. For example, if you are tuning the learning rate and batch size of a neural network, you would specify a range of values for each hyperparameter, and Grid Search would create a grid of all possible combinations to evaluate.

The advantage of Grid Search is that it ensures you search through all specified combinations, leaving no stone unturned in the hyperparameter space. This exhaustive search can be beneficial when you have a small number of hyperparameters to tune and want to find the best combination.

However, a downside of Grid Search is its computational cost. As the number of hyperparameters and their possible values increase, the search space grows exponentially, leading to longer training times and increased computational resources.

Random Search, on the other hand, takes a more probabilistic approach to hyperparameter tuning. Instead of exhaustively searching through all possible combinations, Random Search randomly samples hyperparameters from predefined distributions.

For example, if you are tuning the learning rate, you might specify a uniform distribution between 0.001 and 0.1, and Random Search would randomly select values within this range for each trial.

Random Search is computationally more efficient compared to Grid Search because it doesn't explore every possible combination. Instead, it relies on the law of large numbers to find good hyperparameter settings through random sampling.

The effectiveness of Random Search is based on the assumption that good hyperparameters are not necessarily evenly distributed across the entire search space. In many cases, a few well-chosen random samples can lead to competitive or even superior model performance.

Random Search is particularly useful when dealing with a large hyperparameter search space or when computational resources are limited. It allows you to explore a wide range of hyperparameters without the need for excessive computational power.

One important aspect of both Grid Search and Random Search is the evaluation of the model's performance for each hyperparameter combination. Typically, a performance metric, such as accuracy, precision, recall, or mean squared error, is used to assess how well the model performs with different hyperparameters.

To avoid bias in the evaluation, it's common to use techniques like cross-validation. Cross-validation involves splitting the dataset into multiple subsets, training and testing the model on different subsets, and averaging the performance metrics to obtain a more robust estimate of the model's performance.

Both Grid Search and Random Search can be implemented using libraries like scikit-learn in Python, which provide built-in functions for hyperparameter tuning. These libraries automate the process of trying out different hyperparameters, training models, and evaluating their performance, saving you time and effort.

The choice between Grid Search and Random Search depends on various factors, including the size of the hyperparameter search space, available computational resources, and the desired level of optimization. In practice, it's common to start with Random Search to get a sense of the hyperparameter space and then use Grid Search for a more fine-grained search around promising regions.

It's important to note that hyperparameter tuning is an iterative process. Even after running Grid Search or Random Search, you may need to further refine your model by adjusting hyperparameters based on the results and repeating the process.

Moreover, the effectiveness of hyperparameter tuning can vary from one machine learning problem to another. Some problems may be more sensitive to specific hyperparameters, while others may not benefit significantly from tuning.

In summary, Grid Search and Random Search are two valuable techniques for hyperparameter tuning in machine learning and deep learning. Grid Search explores all possible hyperparameter combinations systematically, while Random Search samples hyperparameters probabilistically.

The choice between these methods depends on factors like the size of the search space and available computational resources. Both approaches help find the best hyperparameter settings for your model, improving its performance and predictive accuracy.

It's worth noting that hyperparameter tuning is just one aspect of model development. Data preprocessing, feature engineering, and model selection also play crucial roles in building effective machine learning models. Bayesian Optimization is an advanced technique used for hyperparameter tuning in machine learning and deep learning. It is particularly useful when the search space for hyperparameters is complex, high-dimensional, or expensive to explore using traditional methods such as Grid Search or Random Search. The fundamental idea behind Bayesian Optimization is to use a probabilistic model to guide the search for optimal hyperparameters. Instead of evaluating all possible hyperparameter combinations, Bayesian Optimization selects promising combinations based on the model's predictions.

The process begins with defining a probabilistic surrogate model, often a Gaussian Process (GP), that models the objective function or the performance metric as a probabilistic distribution. The GP estimates how the performance metric varies with different hyperparameter settings and provides uncertainty estimates for its predictions.

The next step is to choose an acquisition function, which is a heuristic that helps select the next hyperparameter configuration to evaluate. Common acquisition functions include Probability of Improvement (PI), Expected Improvement (EI), and Upper Confidence Bound (UCB).

The acquisition function balances the trade-off between exploration and exploitation. Exploration involves sampling hyperparameters in regions where the model's uncertainty is high, while exploitation focuses on areas where the model predicts better performance.

During the optimization process, Bayesian Optimization iteratively selects a new hyperparameter configuration to evaluate, updates the surrogate model using the observed performance, and repeats this cycle until a stopping criterion is met.

One of the advantages of Bayesian Optimization is its ability to efficiently explore the hyperparameter space by considering both the model's predictions and its uncertainty. This means that it can quickly narrow down the search to promising regions, reducing the number of evaluations needed to find the optimal configuration.

Furthermore, Bayesian Optimization is capable of handling various types of hyperparameters, including continuous, discrete, and categorical, making it versatile for different machine learning tasks.

A key feature of Bayesian Optimization is that it focuses on improving the model's performance directly, rather than treating the hyperparameter tuning as a separate optimization problem. This results in more efficient and effective hyperparameter optimization.

However, Bayesian Optimization does have limitations. It can be computationally expensive when the objective function is computationally intensive or when the search space is large. Additionally, the choice of acquisition function and the parameters of the surrogate model need to be carefully tuned for optimal performance.

Implementing Bayesian Optimization requires specialized libraries like scikit-optimize or BayesianOptimization in Python. These libraries provide easy-to-use interfaces for defining the objective function, specifying hyperparameter search spaces, and setting optimization parameters.

In practice, Bayesian Optimization is an excellent choice for hyperparameter tuning when you want to maximize the performance of your machine learning model while minimizing the number of evaluations. It is particularly useful when the evaluation of the objective function is costly or time-consuming, such as in deep learning tasks where training a single model can take hours or even days. Bayesian Optimization has been successfully applied in various machine learning domains, including computer vision, natural language processing, and reinforcement learning. It has helped researchers and practitioners fine-tune models to achieve state-of-the-art results in many challenging tasks. In summary, Bayesian Optimization is a powerful technique for hyperparameter tuning that leverages probabilistic models and acquisition functions to efficiently explore complex and high-dimensional search spaces. By considering both exploration and exploitation, it guides the search towards optimal hyperparameter configurations while minimizing the number of evaluations. While it may require some computational resources and parameter tuning, Bayesian Optimization is a valuable tool for improving the performance of machine learning models and achieving better results in various applications.

Chapter 3: Advanced Activation Functions

Leaky Rectified Linear Unit (Leaky ReLU) and Parametric Rectified Linear Unit (Parametric ReLU) are variations of the popular activation function known as the Rectified Linear Unit (ReLU). ReLU activation is widely used in neural networks because of its simplicity and effectiveness in mitigating the vanishing gradient problem.

The standard ReLU activation function is defined as $f(x) = \max(0, x)$, which means it replaces all negative input values with zero and leaves positive values unchanged. While ReLU has been successful in many applications, it has a limitation known as the "dying ReLU" problem.

The dying ReLU problem occurs when a neuron becomes inactive during training because it consistently receives negative input values. Once a neuron's output is consistently zero, it no longer contributes to the learning process, leading to a dead or "dying" neuron.

Leaky ReLU was introduced as a solution to the dying ReLU problem. Instead of setting negative input values to zero, Leaky ReLU allows a small, non-zero gradient to flow through, preventing neurons from becoming completely inactive.

Mathematically, Leaky ReLU is defined as $f(x) = \max(\alpha x, x)$, where α is a small positive constant. The value of α is typically chosen to be a small positive number, such as 0.01, which ensures that there is a small, non-zero gradient for negative inputs.

The introduction of the α parameter in Leaky ReLU allows the activation function to handle negative values more gracefully. This ensures that neurons continue to learn and adapt even when they receive predominantly negative input during training.

Leaky ReLU has been shown to address the dying ReLU problem effectively and has become a popular choice in many neural network architectures. It is a simple modification to the standard ReLU activation function that can improve training stability and model performance.

Parametric ReLU takes the idea of addressing the dying ReLU problem a step further. Instead of using a fixed α value as in Leaky ReLU, Parametric ReLU allows the α value to be learned during training.

In Parametric ReLU, the activation function is defined as $f(x) = \alpha x$ for $x < 0$ and $f(x) = x$ for $x \geq 0$, where α is a learnable parameter. During training, the neural network adjusts the value of α along with other model parameters to optimize the overall performance.

The advantage of Parametric ReLU is that it can adapt the amount of leakiness on a per-neuron basis. This means that some neurons may have a larger α value (allowing more negative input values) while others may have a smaller α value, depending on what is most beneficial for the task.

Parametric ReLU is a powerful extension of Leaky ReLU because it allows the neural network to learn the optimal amount of leakiness for each neuron. This adaptability can lead to improved model performance, especially in scenarios where the importance of leakiness varies across different parts of the network.

Both Leaky ReLU and Parametric ReLU have demonstrated their effectiveness in addressing the dying ReLU problem and promoting better training of neural networks. They have been widely adopted in various deep learning architectures and have contributed to the success of many state-of-the-art models.

The choice between Leaky ReLU and Parametric ReLU often depends on the specific task and the complexity of the neural network architecture. In simpler models, Leaky ReLU with a fixed α value may suffice, while in more complex models, Parametric ReLU's ability to learn α can provide a performance advantage.

It's important to note that while Leaky ReLU and Parametric ReLU are effective alternatives to standard ReLU, they are not the only activation functions available. Other activation functions, such as Exponential Linear Unit (ELU) and Scaled Exponential Linear Unit (SELU), have also been proposed to address various challenges in neural network training.

In summary, Leaky ReLU and Parametric ReLU are modifications of the standard ReLU activation function designed to address the dying ReLU problem. Leaky ReLU introduces a small, non-zero gradient for negative inputs, while Parametric ReLU allows the gradient to be learned during training.

Both activation functions have been successful in improving the training stability and performance of neural networks, and their choice depends on the complexity of the model and the specific task at hand. These variations contribute to the versatility and adaptability of activation functions in modern deep learning.

Exponential Linear Units (ELU) and Swish are two relatively recent activation functions in the realm of deep learning that have gained attention for their potential benefits in training neural networks.

Activation functions play a crucial role in deep learning models as they determine the output of a neuron or node in a neural network, thereby influencing the network's ability to learn and generalize from data.

ELU, short for Exponential Linear Unit, is an activation function designed to address some of the limitations of the widely used Rectified Linear Unit (ReLU) and its variants.
ReLU has been popular due to its simplicity and ability to mitigate the vanishing gradient problem, but it has drawbacks, including the "dying ReLU" problem, where neurons can become inactive during training.

ELU overcomes the dying ReLU problem by introducing a smooth, non-zero output for negative inputs.
Mathematically, ELU is defined as $f(x) = x$ if $x \geq 0$ and $f(x) = \alpha * (\exp(x) - 1)$ if $x < 0$, where α is a positive hyperparameter that controls the output for negative values.

The key advantage of ELU is its smoothness, which helps gradients flow smoothly during backpropagation.
This results in faster convergence during training and improved generalization, especially in situations where the input data may contain negative values.

Another interesting property of ELU is that it approaches zero as the input becomes more negative, preventing extreme activations and aiding in the stability of training deep neural networks.

While ELU has demonstrated advantages over ReLU and its variants, it's worth noting that it may not always outperform other activation functions in all scenarios.
The choice of activation function often depends on the specific task, architecture, and empirical experimentation.

Swish is another activation function that has gained attention in the deep learning community due to its promising properties.
It was introduced in the paper "Swish: A Self-Gated Activation Function" by researchers at Google.

Swish is defined as $f(x) = x * sigmoid(x)$, where sigmoid is the logistic sigmoid function.
The key idea behind Swish is the introduction of a gating mechanism using the sigmoid function.

The sigmoid function smoothly transitions between values close to zero for negative inputs and values close to one for positive inputs.
This gating mechanism allows Swish to combine the benefits of both linearity for positive inputs and smoothness for negative inputs.

Swish has been shown to perform well in various deep learning tasks, including image classification, natural language processing, and reinforcement learning.
It often achieves competitive or even state-of-the-art results when compared to other activation functions.

One of the advantages of Swish is its self-gating property, which means that the activation function automatically adapts to the characteristics of the data.
This adaptability can lead to better convergence during training and improved generalization.

However, it's important to note that while Swish has shown promise in practice, its performance can vary depending on factors such as the model architecture, dataset, and specific task.
It may not always outperform other activation functions like ELU or variants of ReLU.

The choice between ELU and Swish, or any other activation function, should be made based on empirical experimentation and a thorough understanding of the neural network's requirements.
Different activation functions may have varying impacts on training dynamics and model performance.

Additionally, it's essential to consider the potential trade-offs, such as computational efficiency and ease of optimization, when selecting an activation function for a specific neural network architecture.

In summary, Exponential Linear Units (ELU) and Swish are two activation functions that have emerged as alternatives to the traditional Rectified Linear Unit (ReLU) in deep learning.
ELU addresses the "dying ReLU" problem by introducing smoothness for negative inputs, while Swish introduces a self-gating mechanism that adapts to the data.

Both activation functions have demonstrated advantages in training deep neural networks and achieving competitive results in various tasks.

However, their performance can be task-dependent, and the choice between them should be based on empirical experimentation and the specific requirements of the neural network architecture.

Chapter 4: Regularization and Dropout Techniques

In the realm of machine learning and deep learning, L1 and L2 regularization are two commonly used techniques to prevent overfitting and improve the generalization of models. Overfitting occurs when a model learns to fit the training data too closely, capturing noise and idiosyncrasies that do not generalize well to unseen data.

L1 regularization, also known as Lasso regularization, and L2 regularization, also known as Ridge regularization, are methods to add a penalty term to the loss function during training. These penalty terms discourage the model from assigning excessive importance to any particular feature or weight, effectively controlling the complexity of the model.

Let's begin with L1 regularization. In L1 regularization, a penalty term is added to the loss function that is proportional to the absolute values of the model's weights. Mathematically, it can be represented as $L1 = \lambda * \Sigma |W_i|$, where λ is the regularization strength, W_i represents the weights of the model, and $\Sigma |W_i|$ calculates the sum of the absolute values of the weights.

The L1 penalty encourages sparsity in the model, meaning that it encourages many of the model's weights to be exactly zero. This results in a simpler and more interpretable model because it selects a subset of the most important features while setting others to zero.

L1 regularization is particularly useful when dealing with high-dimensional data, where many features may not contribute significantly to the model's performance. By promoting sparsity, L1 regularization helps identify and retain the most relevant features while discarding less informative ones.

Now, let's turn our attention to L2 regularization. In L2 regularization, a penalty term is added to the loss function that is proportional to the square of the model's weights. Mathematically, it can be represented as $L2 = \lambda * \Sigma(W_i^2)$, where λ is the regularization strength, W_i represents the weights of the model, and $\Sigma(W_i^2)$ calculates the sum of the squared values of the weights.

The L2 penalty encourages the model's weights to be small but not necessarily zero. This results in a smoother and less sparse model compared to L1 regularization.

L2 regularization is effective at preventing overfitting by controlling the magnitudes of the weights, making it suitable for situations where all features are potentially relevant. It helps reduce the impact of outliers and makes the optimization landscape more well-behaved during training.

Both L1 and L2 regularization can be combined, leading to a technique known as Elastic Net regularization. Elastic Net combines the L1 and L2 penalties by adding them together with separate hyperparameters for each regularization term.

The choice between L1, L2, or Elastic Net regularization depends on the specific problem and the characteristics of the data. L1 regularization is favored when feature selection and sparsity are essential, while L2 regularization is suitable for controlling the magnitudes of weights and smoothing the model.

The regularization strength, represented by the hyperparameter λ, plays a crucial role in controlling the balance between fitting the training data and preventing overfitting. The optimal value of λ often needs to be determined through techniques such as cross-validation.

It's important to note that regularization is not limited to linear models but can be applied to various machine learning algorithms, including neural networks. In neural networks, L1 and L2 regularization are typically added as separate terms to the loss function, promoting sparsity in the weights (L1) or controlling their magnitudes (L2).

In summary, L1 and L2 regularization are techniques used to prevent overfitting and improve the generalization of machine learning models. L1 encourages sparsity by adding a penalty term based on the absolute values of weights, while L2 encourages small weights by penalizing the square of weights.

The choice between L1 and L2 regularization depends on the problem and the desired model characteristics, with Elastic Net providing a hybrid approach. Regularization strength is an important hyperparameter that needs to be carefully tuned to strike the right balance between fitting the data and preventing overfitting.

These techniques have proven valuable in a wide range of machine learning applications, helping to build more robust and generalizable models.

In the ever-evolving field of deep learning and neural networks, innovative techniques continue to emerge, addressing specific challenges and enhancing model performance. Two such techniques are DropConnect and Zoneout, which offer unique solutions to improve the training and performance of neural networks.

DropConnect is a regularization technique that extends the concept of Dropout, a widely used method for preventing overfitting in neural networks. Dropout randomly sets a fraction of the connections between neurons to zero during training, effectively "dropping out" some neurons. This helps prevent co-adaptation of neurons and encourages robust learning.

DropConnect takes this idea further by randomly setting a fraction of the weights (rather than neurons) to zero during each forward and backward pass of training. This means that the connections between neurons are randomly selected and set to zero, providing a form of regularization that encourages the network to be more resilient to variations in input data.

The implementation of DropConnect involves multiplying the weights of the network by a binary mask of 1s and 0s, where 1 indicates an active connection, and 0 indicates a dropped connection. The binary mask is generated randomly for each mini-batch of training data.

One of the advantages of DropConnect is its ability to regularize neural networks effectively while maintaining model architecture. It can be applied to various types of layers in a neural network, including fully connected layers and convolutional layers.

By introducing randomness into the network's weights, DropConnect helps prevent the network from relying too heavily on specific connections, which can lead to overfitting. It encourages the network to learn more general features and exhibit better generalization to unseen data.

Zoneout, on the other hand, is a regularization technique specifically designed for recurrent neural networks (RNNs) and their variants, such as long short-term memory (LSTM) networks and gated recurrent units (GRUs). RNNs are commonly used for sequential data, such as natural language processing tasks or time series analysis.

The challenge with training RNNs is that they are prone to overfitting, and their gradients can vanish or explode during backpropagation through time (BPTT). Zoneout addresses these issues by introducing stochasticity into the hidden states of the RNN during training.

In Zoneout, at each time step of the sequence, a fraction of the elements in the hidden state (or cell state for LSTMs) is randomly set to their previous values, effectively "zoning out" or preserving the previous state. This random dropout of elements in the hidden state helps prevent the model from fitting the noise in the training data too closely and encourages more stable and robust training.

Zoneout is particularly useful when training deep RNNs with many time steps, as it helps combat the vanishing gradient problem and encourages the network to capture long-term dependencies in sequential data.

While DropConnect and Zoneout serve different purposes and are applied to different types of neural networks, they share common principles of introducing randomness or dropout during training to improve generalization and combat overfitting.

It's important to note that the effectiveness of these techniques may vary depending on the specific problem, dataset, and network architecture. As with any regularization technique, the choice of whether to use DropConnect, Zoneout, or other methods should be based on empirical experimentation and an understanding of the model's requirements.

Furthermore, there is ongoing research in the field of deep learning, and new regularization techniques and strategies continue to emerge. The choice of which technique to use depends on the goals of the model and the particular challenges posed by the task at hand.

In summary, DropConnect and Zoneout are innovative regularization techniques that address overfitting and instability during training in neural networks. DropConnect extends Dropout by randomly setting weights to zero, while Zoneout introduces stochasticity into RNN hidden states to combat vanishing gradients and improve sequence modeling.

Both techniques have demonstrated their value in various deep learning applications and serve as examples of how creative approaches can enhance the training and performance of neural networks. Researchers and practitioners continue to explore new regularization methods to push the boundaries of what is possible in deep learning.

Chapter 5: Advanced Loss Functions

In the realm of machine learning, especially in the context of Support Vector Machines (SVMs), the hinge loss function plays a fundamental role in training models for classification tasks. The hinge loss is designed to maximize the margin between classes, making it particularly well-suited for binary classification problems where the goal is to separate data points into two distinct categories.

The idea behind hinge loss is closely tied to SVMs, a class of supervised learning algorithms used for both classification and regression tasks. SVMs aim to find a hyperplane that best separates data points of different classes while maximizing the margin, which is the distance between the hyperplane and the nearest data points from each class.

To achieve this goal, SVMs introduce the concept of a margin constraint, where data points are assigned a margin value based on their distance from the decision boundary (hyperplane). The margin constraint ensures that data points are correctly classified with a margin of at least 1, which means they must fall on the correct side of the decision boundary by at least one unit.

The hinge loss function quantifies the violation of this margin constraint for each data point. It assigns a penalty when a data point falls inside the margin or on the wrong side of the decision boundary, and this penalty increases as the distance from the margin constraint increases.

Mathematically, the hinge loss for a single data point is defined as $L(y, f(x)) = \max(0, 1 - y * f(x))$, where y represents the true class label (either +1 or -1), $f(x)$ is the predicted score or decision function, and L(y, f(x)) is the loss for that data point.

The hinge loss has several important properties that make it well-suited for SVMs and binary classification tasks. First, it is a convex and piecewise-linear function, which means it is amenable to convex optimization techniques used to find the optimal hyperplane.

Second, the hinge loss encourages a large margin between classes by penalizing data points that are close to the decision boundary but still correctly classified. Data points that are correctly classified and have a margin of at least 1 do not contribute to the loss, which is a key characteristic of the hinge loss.

Third, the hinge loss is hinge-like in shape, with a "hinge" point at $1 - y * f(x)$. For data points with a margin violation (i.e., $1 - y * f(x) < 0$), the loss increases linearly with the violation, which encourages the model to correct its predictions.

The hinge loss is also known for its robustness to outliers. Since it only assigns a non-zero loss to data points that are misclassified or close to the decision boundary, outliers that are far from the decision boundary have little impact on the loss.

Training an SVM using hinge loss involves finding the hyperplane that minimizes the sum of hinge losses across all data points while satisfying the margin constraint. This optimization problem can be solved using various techniques, including quadratic programming, gradient descent, or specialized algorithms for large-scale problems.

In practice, SVMs with hinge loss are widely used for binary classification tasks, such as image classification, text classification, and bioinformatics. They have demonstrated strong performance and are known for their ability to handle high-dimensional data effectively.

It's important to note that while hinge loss is primarily associated with SVMs, it can also be used as a loss function for other models, such as logistic regression and neural networks, where its margin-maximizing properties can be advantageous.

In summary, hinge loss is a fundamental loss function used in Support Vector Machines (SVMs) for binary classification tasks. It quantifies the violation of a margin constraint and encourages the model to find a hyperplane that maximizes the margin between classes.

The hinge loss is known for its convexity, margin-maximizing properties, and robustness to outliers, making it a valuable tool in machine learning for a wide range of applications. Training SVMs with hinge loss involves optimizing the model's parameters to minimize the sum of hinge losses while ensuring correct classification and margin constraints are met.

In the realm of deep learning and neural networks, Siamese networks are a class of models designed for tasks like image similarity and one-shot learning. These networks consist of twin subnetworks with shared weights, and they are particularly useful for scenarios where you need to compare and measure the similarity between pairs of input data.

One of the key components of training Siamese networks is the contrastive loss function, which is specifically designed to encourage the network to learn embeddings such that similar inputs are closer in the embedding space, while dissimilar inputs are pushed apart. This notion of embedding space proximity is central to many similarity-based tasks, including face recognition, signature verification, and more.

The contrastive loss function aims to minimize the distance between embeddings of similar pairs and maximize the distance between embeddings of dissimilar pairs. In other words, it enforces that similar pairs are pulled together in the embedding space, while dissimilar pairs are pushed apart.

Mathematically, the contrastive loss can be defined as $L(y, d) = (1 - y) * (d^2) + y * \max(\text{margin} - d, 0)^2$, where:

$L(y, d)$ represents the contrastive loss for a pair of inputs, with y being the binary label indicating whether the pair is similar ($y = 0$) or dissimilar ($y = 1$).

d represents the Euclidean distance or another suitable distance metric between the embeddings of the pair.

The margin parameter controls how much distance should be enforced between dissimilar pairs.

Let's break down the components of this loss function:

The first term, $(1 - y) * (d^2)$, is responsible for pulling similar pairs ($y = 0$) closer together by minimizing the squared distance between their embeddings (d^2).

The second term, $y * \max(\text{margin} - d, 0)^2$, focuses on pushing dissimilar pairs ($y = 1$) apart. It computes the squared distance between their embeddings, but only if the distance is less than the specified margin. Otherwise, it contributes zero to the loss.

The margin parameter is a critical hyperparameter in contrastive loss, and its value determines the trade-off between embedding similarity for similar pairs and separation for dissimilar pairs. A larger margin enforces stricter separation, while a smaller margin allows similar pairs to be closer in the embedding space.

During training, the Siamese network learns to adjust its weights to minimize this contrastive loss, effectively optimizing the embedding space to satisfy the desired constraints.

Siamese networks with contrastive loss have proven to be effective in various tasks where measuring similarity between pairs of data is crucial. For instance, in face recognition, Siamese networks can be trained to embed facial images in such a way that faces of the same person are close together in the embedding space, facilitating accurate recognition.

One of the advantages of using contrastive loss in Siamese networks is that it allows for training with pairs of data, making it suitable for tasks where obtaining labeled data is challenging. By comparing pairs of data points and optimizing the embeddings accordingly, Siamese networks can learn to generalize well even with limited labeled examples.

Additionally, Siamese networks and contrastive loss can be extended to triplet loss, where each training sample consists of an anchor, a positive (similar) example, and a negative (dissimilar) example. In triplet loss, the network is encouraged to make the distance between the anchor and the positive example smaller than the distance between the anchor and the negative example by at least a margin.

In summary, contrastive loss plays a crucial role in training Siamese networks for similarity-based tasks. It encourages the network to learn embeddings that bring similar inputs closer together in the embedding space while pushing dissimilar inputs apart.

The margin hyperparameter in contrastive loss controls the trade-off between similarity and separation, and Siamese networks with contrastive loss have demonstrated their effectiveness in various applications, from face recognition to one-shot learning, where comparing and measuring similarity between data pairs is essential.

Chapter 6: Custom Layers and Model Extensions

In the world of neural networks and deep learning, the activation function is a crucial component that introduces non-linearity into the model, allowing it to learn complex relationships within the data. While standard activation functions like the sigmoid, hyperbolic tangent (tanh), and rectified linear unit (ReLU) are commonly used, there are situations where custom activation functions can be beneficial.

Custom activation functions, also known as non-standard or exotic activation functions, are functions that deviate from the traditional choices and are designed to address specific challenges or to capture unique characteristics of certain data. Building custom activation functions can be a creative and powerful way to enhance the expressiveness of neural networks and tailor them to particular tasks.

The primary purpose of an activation function is to introduce non-linearity into the network, enabling it to approximate complex functions. Non-linearity is essential because real-world data often exhibits intricate patterns and relationships that cannot be captured by linear models.

One of the simplest and most well-known activation functions is the sigmoid function. It maps input values to the range (0, 1) and is commonly used in the hidden layers of feedforward neural networks. However, the sigmoid function has its limitations, such as vanishing gradients for extreme input values, which can hinder training deep networks.

The hyperbolic tangent (tanh) function is another popular choice that maps input values to the range (-1, 1). While it mitigates some of the vanishing gradient issues of the sigmoid, it still suffers from the problem to some extent.

Rectified linear unit (ReLU) has gained significant popularity in recent years. It replaces negative input values with zero, introducing non-linearity and mitigating vanishing gradient problems for positive inputs. ReLU and its variants like Leaky ReLU and Parametric ReLU have proven effective in many deep learning applications.

However, there are scenarios where custom activation functions can outperform these standard choices. For example, when dealing with specific data distributions or optimization challenges, designing a custom activation function tailored to the problem at hand can lead to better results.

Designing a custom activation function requires a good understanding of the data and problem domain. It involves defining a mathematical function that transforms the input data into a desired range while introducing the necessary non-linearity. This function should be differentiable, as gradients are essential for training neural networks using backpropagation.

A common approach to designing custom activation functions is to combine multiple elementary functions to create a composite function. For instance, you might create a custom activation function that smoothly transitions from a sigmoid-like shape for small input values to a linear behavior for larger values.

Another approach is to use piecewise-defined functions, where different functions are applied to different input ranges. This can be useful for modeling data with different characteristics in different regions.

Additionally, you can leverage domain-specific knowledge to design custom activation functions. For example, in image processing tasks, you might create an activation function that enhances certain features in the data.

Implementing a custom activation function in a neural network framework like TensorFlow or PyTorch involves defining the function in code and ensuring it is differentiable. You can then use this custom activation function like any standard activation function when defining the layers of your neural network.

While designing and implementing custom activation functions can be a creative and effective approach, it also comes with challenges. One challenge is ensuring that the custom function does not introduce numerical instability or convergence issues during training.

Another challenge is that custom activation functions may require careful tuning of hyperparameters, such as learning rates and initialization methods, to achieve optimal performance.

In summary, custom activation functions are a powerful tool in the toolkit of deep learning practitioners. They allow for the design of activation functions tailored to specific data characteristics and problem domains.

While standard activation functions like sigmoid, tanh, and ReLU are widely used and effective in many cases, custom activation functions can provide a competitive advantage when dealing with unique challenges or opportunities in machine learning and neural network applications.

In the field of deep learning and natural language

processing, attention mechanisms have emerged as a powerful tool for improving the performance of various neural network architectures. Attention mechanisms enable models to focus on specific parts of input sequences, allowing them to selectively weigh the importance of different elements, and this has proven highly effective in tasks like machine translation, text summarization, image captioning, and more.

At its core, an attention mechanism is a mechanism that helps a neural network "pay attention" to relevant information while processing sequences of data. It allows the network to dynamically weigh the importance of different parts of the input when generating an output, making it a valuable addition to models that deal with variable-length sequences.

One of the most well-known attention mechanisms is the Transformer, a neural network architecture introduced in the paper "Attention Is All You Need" by Vaswani et al. in 2017. The Transformer architecture revolutionized natural language processing and machine translation by introducing a self-attention mechanism that enables the model to consider dependencies between words in a sentence without relying on recurrent or convolutional layers.

The core idea behind the self-attention mechanism is to compute attention scores between all pairs of words in a sentence, allowing each word to attend to others based on their semantic relevance. These attention scores are used to create weighted representations of words, which capture their contextual information in the sentence.

The self-attention mechanism operates in three main steps:

Compute the Query, Key, and Value vectors for each word in the input sequence. These vectors are linear transformations of the original word embeddings.

Calculate attention scores by taking the dot product of the Query vector of a word with the Key vectors of all other words in the sequence. These scores represent how much attention each word should pay to the current word.

Use the attention scores to weight the Value vectors of all words and compute a weighted sum. This produces the context vector for each word, capturing its context in relation to all other words in the sequence.

The Transformer architecture also introduced the concept of multi-head attention, where multiple sets of Query, Key, and Value transformations are applied in parallel. This allows the model to learn different types of attention, capturing various types of relationships and dependencies in the data.

Attention mechanisms have since been adopted in various neural network architectures beyond the Transformer. For instance, in the field of computer vision, the Vision Transformer (ViT) applies self-attention to image patches, enabling it to achieve state-of-the-art performance in image classification tasks.

Implementing attention mechanisms in neural network frameworks like TensorFlow or PyTorch involves defining the attention mechanism layer, which can be incorporated into a broader model. The layer typically accepts input tensors and computes attention scores and context vectors as described earlier.

One of the advantages of attention mechanisms is their ability to handle sequences of variable length. Unlike recurrent neural networks (RNNs), which suffer from vanishing gradients and slow training for long sequences, attention mechanisms can efficiently process long sequences in parallel, making them suitable for tasks involving lengthy texts or sequences.

Moreover, attention mechanisms offer interpretability, as they provide insight into which parts of the input are most important for generating specific outputs. This can be valuable in applications where model interpretability and transparency are crucial.

There are different variations of attention mechanisms, including:

Self-Attention: As discussed earlier, self-attention mechanisms allow words in a sequence to attend to each other's contextual information.

Cross-Attention: In tasks involving multiple sequences, such as machine translation, cross-attention mechanisms enable one sequence to attend to the other while generating output.

Global Average Pooling Attention: This attention mechanism computes a weighted average of all input elements, effectively summarizing the entire input sequence.

Content-Based Attention: This type of attention focuses on the content of the input, aligning elements with similar content.

Location-Based Attention: Location-based attention aligns elements based on their positions in the input sequence, which can be useful in tasks like text summarization.

Implementing attention mechanisms requires careful consideration of hyperparameters, including the number of attention heads, the dimensionality of Query, Key, and Value vectors, and the choice of activation functions.

In summary, attention mechanisms have significantly advanced the capabilities of neural networks in various natural language processing, computer vision, and sequence modeling tasks. Their ability to selectively attend to relevant information in sequences has made them a fundamental component of modern deep learning architectures.

Implementing attention mechanisms in neural networks involves defining layers that compute attention scores and context vectors, which can be incorporated into models to improve their performance.

Attention mechanisms offer advantages such as handling variable-length sequences efficiently, providing interpretability, and achieving state-of-the-art results in a wide range of applications, making them a vital tool in the deep learning practitioner's toolkit.

Chapter 7: Interpretability and Explainability in Neural Networks

Feature importance analysis is a fundamental aspect of machine learning and data analysis, providing valuable insights into the predictive power of different features in a dataset. Understanding which features have the most significant impact on a model's predictions can help in model selection, feature engineering, and domain-specific decision-making.

One common approach to assess feature importance is to use techniques like feature importance scores, permutation importance, and SHAP (SHapley Additive exPlanations) values. These methods can be applied to various machine learning algorithms, including decision trees, random forests, gradient boosting, and linear models.

Feature importance scores are a straightforward way to gauge the contribution of each feature in a machine learning model. For example, in decision tree-based models, features that are frequently used for splitting nodes tend to have higher importance scores. Random forests and gradient boosting algorithms extend this idea by aggregating the feature importance scores from multiple trees to provide a more robust estimate of feature importance.

Permutation importance is another useful technique for assessing feature importance. It involves randomly shuffling the values of a single feature while keeping the others unchanged and measuring the impact on the model's performance. If a feature is crucial, permuting it should significantly degrade the model's predictive ability, resulting in a noticeable drop in performance metrics like accuracy or mean squared error.

SHAP values, on the other hand, offer a more nuanced view of feature importance. They are based on cooperative game theory and provide a way to attribute the contribution of each feature to a specific prediction. SHAP values consider interactions between features and can reveal whether a feature has a positive or negative impact on a prediction. These values can be visualized using SHAP summary plots or individual SHAP value plots, which provide insights into the overall model behavior and the impact of specific features on individual predictions.

In practice, feature importance analysis can help data scientists and machine learning practitioners make informed decisions about feature selection, model refinement, and problem understanding. For instance, if a model heavily relies on a particular feature, it might be essential to ensure the feature is reliable, up-to-date, and relevant to the problem at hand. Additionally, feature importance analysis can highlight redundant or irrelevant features that can be safely removed from the dataset, simplifying the model and potentially improving its generalization.

While feature importance analysis is a valuable tool, it is essential to interpret the results within the context of the specific problem and model. Not all feature importance techniques are equally suitable for every situation. For example, permutation importance can be computationally expensive for models with a large number of features, and SHAP values may not be interpretable in some cases.

It's crucial to keep in mind that feature importance analysis is not a silver bullet. It does not provide causal relationships between features and predictions but rather quantifies the associations. In some cases, the most important features may not be actionable or may not have a straightforward interpretation.

Additionally, feature importance analysis is subject to the limitations of the underlying machine learning algorithms. For example, linear models may not capture complex interactions between features, while decision tree-based models can produce biased feature importance scores for categorical variables with many categories.

In summary, feature importance analysis is a powerful technique for understanding the importance of different features in machine learning models. It can guide feature engineering efforts, improve model interpretability, and inform decision-making. However, it should be used judiciously, considering the specific problem, model, and limitations of the chosen feature importance technique.

LIME (Local Interpretable Model-agnostic Explanations) and SHAP (SHapley Additive exPlanations) are two prominent explainability methods in the field of machine learning, designed to provide insights into the predictions of complex models. They play a crucial role in addressing the "black box" nature of many machine learning algorithms, allowing us to understand why a particular model makes certain predictions.

LIME is a model-agnostic approach that focuses on explaining individual predictions. It does this by approximating the behavior of the complex model locally, around a specific instance of interest. The primary idea behind LIME is to create a simplified, interpretable model, often a linear or decision tree model, that closely mimics the predictions of the original model for a given data point.

LIME operates as follows:

Select a data point for which you want an explanation.

Perturb the data point by introducing slight random variations.

Observe how the complex model's predictions change for the perturbed data points.

Fit a simple interpretable model to the perturbed data points and their corresponding predictions.

Use the interpretable model to explain the complex model's behavior for the selected instance.

LIME provides local explanations, meaning it explains individual predictions rather than the entire model. This approach makes LIME particularly valuable for understanding why a specific instance received a particular prediction, which can be crucial for building trust in machine learning systems and diagnosing model errors.

On the other hand, SHAP is a more comprehensive method that offers both local and global insights into model predictions. SHAP values are based on cooperative game theory and aim to attribute the contribution of each feature to a prediction.

The core concept behind SHAP is the Shapley value, which calculates the average marginal contribution of each feature to all possible coalitions of features. In the context of machine learning, a feature's Shapley value represents its contribution to a prediction relative to the average contribution of all features.

SHAP values can be used to explain individual predictions as well as provide global insights into the model's behavior. For individual predictions, SHAP values reveal how each feature influenced a specific prediction. For global understanding, aggregating SHAP values across a dataset can highlight which features consistently have the most substantial impact on predictions.

SHAP values can be visualized in various ways, including summary plots, individual feature importance plots, and dependency plots. These visualizations help users interpret the importance and directionality of features in a model.

While both LIME and SHAP are powerful tools for model explanation, they have different strengths and weaknesses. LIME is often more computationally efficient and is useful for explaining complex models quickly. However, it might not provide as detailed global insights as SHAP.

In contrast, SHAP offers a more complete picture of feature importance at both the local and global levels. However, it can be computationally expensive, especially for models with many features or when explaining many instances.

Additionally, the choice between LIME and SHAP may depend on the specific use case and the interpretability needs of the user. LIME's local explanations are suitable for debugging individual predictions and gaining trust in specific decisions, while SHAP's global insights are valuable for understanding overall model behavior and feature importance.

To implement LIME and SHAP, you can use existing libraries and packages in Python, such as lime and shap.

These libraries provide straightforward interfaces for explaining models and visualizing the results.

In summary, LIME and SHAP are essential tools in the toolbox of machine learning practitioners and data scientists. They offer valuable insights into complex model predictions and help bridge the gap between machine learning models and human understanding.

By using these explainability methods, users can gain confidence in their models, diagnose issues, and make informed decisions about feature engineering, model selection, and model deployment.

Chapter 8: Autoencoders and Variational Autoencoders (VAEs)

Denoising Autoencoders (DAEs) are a type of artificial neural network that has found significant use in various machine learning tasks, particularly in unsupervised learning and dimensionality reduction. These neural networks are part of the broader family of autoencoders, which are designed to encode and decode data, ultimately learning a compressed representation of the input.

The primary goal of DAEs is to remove noise or unwanted variations from data while preserving essential features. They achieve this by training the network to map noisy data to its clean or noise-free version. This process helps in feature extraction, data denoising, and improving the robustness of downstream tasks.

The architecture of a DAE closely resembles that of a standard autoencoder. It consists of an encoder network, a bottleneck layer, and a decoder network. The encoder takes the input data and maps it to a lower-dimensional representation in the bottleneck layer, while the decoder attempts to reconstruct the original input from this compressed representation.

The key difference between a DAE and a standard autoencoder lies in the training process. In a DAE, the training data is intentionally corrupted by adding noise or introducing variations. This noisy data is then used as the input, and the network is trained to produce clean data as the output. The objective is to minimize the reconstruction error, encouraging the network to learn a robust representation that can remove noise from corrupted inputs.

The noise introduced during training can take various forms, such as Gaussian noise, dropout, or other types of perturbations. The choice of noise type depends on the specific problem and the nature of the data. For example, in image denoising tasks, Gaussian noise may be added to the pixel values of images.

One of the advantages of DAEs is their ability to learn meaningful representations of data without requiring labeled examples. This unsupervised learning approach makes DAEs particularly useful for tasks where obtaining labeled data is expensive or challenging. They can capture underlying patterns and structures in the data, even when the data is noisy or exhibits complex variations.

Another use case for DAEs is in dimensionality reduction and feature extraction. By training a DAE on high-dimensional data and using the encoder network to obtain the bottleneck representation, it is possible to reduce the dimensionality of the data while retaining relevant information. This lower-dimensional representation can then be fed into downstream machine learning models for various tasks, such as classification or clustering.

Denoising Autoencoders have been applied in various domains, including image denoising, speech recognition, and natural language processing. In image denoising, DAEs can learn to remove noise from images, making them cleaner and more suitable for computer vision tasks. Similarly, in speech recognition, DAEs can help remove background noise from audio signals, improving the accuracy of speech recognition systems.

In natural language processing, DAEs can be applied to text data for tasks such as text denoising, where they learn to clean noisy or corrupted text data, making it more suitable for language modeling or sentiment analysis. DAEs can also be used for feature extraction from text data, capturing meaningful representations of words or phrases.

Training a Denoising Autoencoder involves optimizing the network's parameters to minimize the reconstruction error between the noisy input and the clean output. This optimization process typically employs gradient descent-based algorithms, such as stochastic gradient descent (SGD) or Adam, to update the network's weights and biases iteratively. The objective is to find the optimal set of weights that enable the network to remove noise effectively while preserving essential information.

Regularization techniques, such as dropout or L1/L2 regularization, can also be applied to prevent overfitting during training. These techniques help the network generalize better to unseen data and improve its ability to denoise noisy inputs.

In summary, Denoising Autoencoders are a valuable tool in machine learning for data denoising, dimensionality reduction, and feature extraction. They learn to remove noise and variations from data, making it cleaner and more suitable for downstream tasks. Their unsupervised learning approach and flexibility in handling various types of data noise make them a versatile choice in many applications across different domains.

Variational Autoencoders (VAEs) represent a fascinating development in the realm of generative modeling and have gained significant attention in recent years for their ability to generate high-quality images. These models combine elements of both autoencoders and probabilistic graphical models, allowing them to generate new data samples that closely resemble those in the training dataset.

Implementing VAEs for image generation is an exciting journey that involves understanding the core concepts, designing the architecture, and training the model effectively.

At the heart of VAEs is the idea of encoding and decoding data in a probabilistic manner. Instead of mapping data directly to a fixed-dimensional representation as traditional autoencoders do, VAEs map data to a probability distribution in a latent space. This probabilistic encoding enables VAEs to generate not just one fixed output for each input but rather a range of possible outputs.

To start implementing a VAE for image generation, the first step is defining the architecture. A typical VAE consists of an encoder network, a bottleneck layer where the probabilistic encoding happens, and a decoder network. The encoder network takes an input image and encodes it into the parameters of a probability distribution, usually a multivariate Gaussian distribution.

The encoder network's output includes both the mean and the variance of the distribution in the latent space. These parameters are crucial because they determine the shape of the distribution, which is essential for generating samples.

The latent space, often called the "z-space," is where the magic of VAEs happens. It represents a lower-dimensional space where data is probabilistically encoded. By sampling from this latent space, new data samples can be generated, a process known as "decoding."

The decoder network takes samples from the latent space and maps them back to the original data space, in this case, images. The decoder's output should resemble the input images, and its architecture can be symmetric to the encoder network.

During training, the VAE optimizes two key objectives: the reconstruction loss and the regularization term. The reconstruction loss measures how well the decoder can reconstruct the input data from samples in the latent space. Common choices for this loss include mean squared error or binary cross-entropy, depending on the nature of the data.

The regularization term encourages the latent space to follow a specific structure. In VAEs, this is typically achieved by adding a term to the loss function that encourages the latent space to resemble a multivariate Gaussian distribution with mean zero and unit variance. This regularization term is essential for ensuring that the latent space is continuous and interpretable.

Training a VAE requires careful consideration of hyperparameters, including the dimensionality of the latent space, the choice of activation functions, and the learning rate. These hyperparameters can significantly impact the quality of the generated images and the model's convergence.

One crucial aspect of VAEs is the trade-off between the reconstruction loss and the regularization term. If the regularization term dominates the loss, the latent space may be overly constrained, leading to less varied and less interesting generated images. Conversely, if the reconstruction loss dominates, the latent space may not be well-structured, resulting in less control over the generated samples.

The key to achieving high-quality image generation with VAEs is to strike the right balance between these two objectives. This balance can often be fine-tuned during training by adjusting the weight of the regularization term. A powerful feature of VAEs is their ability to perform latent space manipulations. By navigating the latent space, it's possible to generate new images with specific characteristics. For example, by interpolating between two points in the latent space, you can smoothly transition between different image styles or attributes.

Implementing such latent space manipulations requires a good understanding of the latent space's structure and careful design of experiments to explore it effectively.

When deploying a VAE for image generation, it's essential to ensure that the model's quality meets the application's requirements. This may involve fine-tuning the model, increasing the dimensionality of the latent space, or adjusting other hyperparameters to generate images that align with the desired style or content.

In summary, implementing VAEs for image generation is a fascinating and rewarding endeavor. These models combine the power of probabilistic encoding with neural networks to generate diverse and high-quality images. Understanding the core principles, designing an appropriate architecture, and effectively training the model are essential steps in harnessing the creative potential of VAEs for image generation.

Chapter 9: Sequence-to-Sequence Models and Transformers

Encoder-Decoder architectures have become a cornerstone in the field of deep learning and have found applications in a wide range of tasks, from machine translation and image captioning to speech recognition and image generation. These architectures are designed to handle sequences of data and are particularly well-suited for tasks where an input sequence needs to be transformed into an output sequence of potentially different lengths.

The fundamental idea behind encoder-decoder architectures is to use two separate neural networks, one known as the encoder and the other as the decoder. The encoder takes in the input data, which can be a sequence of symbols, images, or any other structured data, and transforms it into a fixed-length representation called the "context" or "latent" vector.

This context vector captures essential information from the input data, often in a compressed or abstract form. The encoder's role is to learn how to encode the input data into a representation that preserves the information needed for the task at hand. This encoding should ideally be robust to variations in the input and contain relevant features for generating the desired output.

Once the encoder has created the context vector, the decoder network comes into play. The decoder's job is to take this context vector and generate an output sequence from it. This output sequence can be of variable length and can belong to a different domain or modality than the input.

The decoder is trained to produce sequences that are coherent and relevant to the task, such as translating a sentence from one language to another or generating a detailed caption for an image. In essence, the decoder learns how to "decode" the context vector into an output sequence that serves the desired purpose.

One of the key challenges in encoder-decoder architectures is determining how to bridge the gap between the encoder's fixed-length context vector and the variable-length output sequence. This requires careful design of the decoder network, including the choice of recurrent or attention mechanisms, which are crucial for maintaining coherence and handling sequences of different lengths.

Recurrent neural networks (RNNs) have historically been a popular choice for the decoder's architecture. RNNs can generate sequences one element at a time, conditioning each step on the previously generated elements and the context vector. However, they have limitations, such as difficulty in capturing long-range dependencies and a tendency to suffer from vanishing gradients during training.

To address some of these limitations, attention mechanisms have emerged as a powerful addition to encoder-decoder architectures. Attention mechanisms allow the decoder to focus on different parts of the input sequence when generating each element of the output sequence. This attention to relevant input information has significantly improved the quality of generated sequences and the ability to handle longer sequences.

In machine translation, for example, attention mechanisms have enabled models to effectively align words in the source and target languages, leading to more accurate translations. Similarly, in image captioning, attention mechanisms allow the model to focus on different regions of the image as it generates each word of the caption, resulting in more descriptive and contextually relevant captions.

Another important consideration in encoder-decoder architectures is the training process. These models are typically trained using a variant of the teacher-forcing technique, where the ground-truth output is provided as input to the decoder during training. This approach helps stabilize training but can lead to issues during inference when the model needs to generate sequences autonomously.

To mitigate this problem, techniques like scheduled sampling and reinforcement learning have been proposed to bridge the gap between training and inference and improve the quality of generated sequences.

Encoder-decoder architectures have been applied to various domains and tasks. In addition to machine translation and image captioning, they have been used for speech recognition, where the input is an audio waveform, and the output is a sequence of phonemes or words. They have also found applications in text summarization, where the goal is to generate a concise summary of a longer text.

Furthermore, encoder-decoder architectures have been used in image-to-image translation tasks, such as image segmentation, where the input is an image, and the output is a pixel-wise labeling of objects. In this case, the encoder extracts features from the input image, and the decoder generates a corresponding output image with the desired labels.

In summary, encoder-decoder architectures have become a versatile tool for handling sequence-to-sequence tasks in deep learning. They have shown remarkable success in various applications, thanks to their ability to capture complex relationships between input and output sequences. As research in this field continues to evolve, encoder-decoder architectures are likely to play an even more significant role in solving challenging problems across different domains.

The Transformer architecture has revolutionized Natural Language Processing (NLP) tasks and has become the foundation for many state-of-the-art models, including BERT, GPT, and their variants. Introduced in the paper "Attention Is All You Need" by Vaswani et al. in 2017, the Transformer architecture introduced a novel way of processing sequential data, which has since become a game-changer in the field of NLP.

At the core of the Transformer architecture is the concept of self-attention, which enables the model to weigh the importance of different parts of an input sequence when making predictions. This self-attention mechanism allows the model to capture long-range dependencies in the data, making it highly effective for tasks that involve understanding context and relationships in text.

Unlike traditional recurrent neural networks (RNNs) and convolutional neural networks (CNNs), which process sequences step by step or with fixed-sized windows, the Transformer processes the entire sequence in parallel, significantly speeding up training and inference. This parallelization is achieved through self-attention layers, which compute attention scores between all pairs of positions in the input sequence.

The Transformer architecture consists of an encoder and a decoder, both of which contain multiple layers of self-attention and feedforward sublayers. The encoder processes the input sequence, while the decoder generates the output sequence, making it suitable for sequence-to-sequence tasks like machine translation or text summarization.

Each self-attention layer in the Transformer computes a weighted sum of all input positions, where the weights are determined by the attention scores. These attention scores are learned during training and allow the model to assign higher weights to relevant positions in the input sequence. This attention mechanism enables the model to focus on the context that matters most for a given prediction, which is especially valuable for NLP tasks involving language understanding and generation.

In addition to self-attention layers, the Transformer architecture includes feedforward sublayers, which apply a simple, fully connected neural network to each position in the sequence independently. These sublayers help the model capture complex relationships within the data and provide flexibility in modeling different types of patterns.

One of the strengths of the Transformer architecture is its ability to be scaled up. By increasing the number of layers and attention heads in the model, Transformer-based models can handle large-scale datasets and learn complex patterns effectively. This scalability has been a driving force behind the success of models like BERT and GPT-3, which have achieved remarkable results on various NLP benchmarks.

Another key innovation introduced by the Transformer architecture is positional encoding. Since the model does not have any inherent notion of order in the input sequence, positional encodings are added to the input embeddings to provide information about the positions of tokens. These positional encodings are learned and contribute to the model's ability to understand the sequential nature of the data.

The Transformer architecture has had a significant impact on various NLP tasks. For example, BERT (Bidirectional Encoder Representations from Transformers) pre-trained models have set new standards in tasks like text classification, named entity recognition, and sentiment analysis by providing context-aware embeddings for text.

On the other hand, GPT (Generative Pre-trained Transformer) models have excelled in text generation tasks, including language modeling, text completion, and story generation. GPT-3, in particular, with its 175 billion parameters, has demonstrated the ability to generate coherent and contextually relevant text, showcasing the power of the Transformer architecture.

Fine-tuning pre-trained Transformer models for specific NLP tasks has become a common practice. This involves training the model on a smaller, task-specific dataset while initializing its weights with pre-trained weights from a larger model. Fine-tuning leverages the general language understanding capabilities of the pre-trained model and adapts it to the specific task at hand.

The Transformer architecture's success extends beyond English-language tasks, as it has been adapted to many other languages and achieved state-of-the-art results in machine translation, language modeling, and more. Multilingual models like mBERT (Multilingual BERT) have shown the ability to handle multiple languages effectively, making them valuable tools in a globalized world.

In summary, the Transformer architecture has fundamentally transformed the landscape of Natural Language Processing. Its innovative self-attention mechanism, parallel processing, and scalability have enabled it to achieve outstanding results across a wide range of NLP tasks. As research in NLP continues to evolve, the Transformer architecture remains at the forefront of innovation, driving advancements in language understanding and generation.

Chapter 10: Cutting-Edge AI Applications and Future Trends

Quantum neural networks represent a fascinating intersection of quantum computing and machine learning, promising the potential to solve complex problems that are currently intractable for classical computers.

These networks harness the unique properties of quantum bits, or qubits, which can exist in multiple states simultaneously due to superposition.

This property enables quantum neural networks to explore vast solution spaces in parallel, providing a significant advantage in optimization and search problems.

Quantum neural networks can be divided into several categories, including quantum versions of classical neural networks, quantum Boltzmann machines, and quantum circuits designed specifically for machine learning tasks.

One of the most well-known quantum neural network models is the Quantum Hopfield Network, which extends the classical Hopfield network to utilize quantum superposition and entanglement.

Quantum Hopfield Networks have shown promise in solving optimization problems, including the traveling salesman problem and graph coloring.

Quantum neural networks also leverage another essential quantum property called entanglement, where the state of one qubit is dependent on the state of another, even when separated by large distances.

This property can be harnessed to build quantum neural networks that can efficiently represent and manipulate complex data relationships.

Quantum Boltzmann machines, a quantum counterpart to classical Boltzmann machines, use quantum annealers or quantum circuits to perform probabilistic sampling and optimization tasks.

These models have demonstrated potential in solving combinatorial optimization problems, such as the Ising model, with quantum advantages.

Quantum circuits designed for machine learning tasks are another area of active research, with quantum gates specifically tailored for tasks like quantum support vector machines and quantum deep learning.

Quantum neural networks also benefit from quantum interference, where quantum states can constructively or destructively interfere, leading to enhanced computational capabilities.

Quantum interference plays a crucial role in quantum algorithms, such as quantum amplitude amplification, which can be employed to accelerate search and optimization tasks.

One of the major challenges in quantum neural networks is the need for quantum hardware, which is still in the early stages of development.

Quantum computers are highly sensitive to noise and errors, and building large-scale, error-corrected quantum processors remains a significant technological hurdle.

As quantum hardware matures, it is expected that quantum neural networks will become increasingly practical for real-world applications.

Quantum neural networks have the potential to revolutionize fields like cryptography, drug discovery, and optimization by solving problems that were previously considered unsolvable in a reasonable amount of time.

Quantum machine learning algorithms, including quantum neural networks, are being actively researched to leverage quantum computing power for a wide range of applications.

Quantum neural networks could find applications in financial modeling, where complex risk assessment and portfolio optimization problems can benefit from the quantum advantage in handling large datasets and performing efficient optimization.

The healthcare industry could also benefit from quantum neural networks, with applications in drug discovery, genomics, and medical image analysis, where quantum computing can accelerate the search for new drugs and improve disease diagnosis and treatment.

Quantum neural networks are not limited to data analysis tasks; they can also find applications in robotics, natural language processing, and quantum-enhanced sensor technologies.

Despite their potential, quantum neural networks are still in the early stages of development, and many technical challenges must be overcome before they become practical for widespread use.

Quantum error correction, improved qubit coherence times, and the development of specialized quantum hardware are all essential components in realizing the full potential of quantum neural networks.

Quantum neural networks also require dedicated quantum algorithms and software frameworks to enable researchers and developers to harness their power effectively.

In summary, quantum neural networks represent an exciting frontier in the field of machine learning, offering the potential to solve complex problems that were previously out of reach for classical computers.

While many challenges remain, the ongoing research and development in quantum computing and quantum machine learning promise a future where quantum neural networks play a significant role in addressing some of the most pressing challenges in science, technology, and industry.

Edge computing is a paradigm that brings computation and data storage closer to the location where it is needed, reducing latency and bandwidth usage, and AI plays a crucial role in making edge devices smarter and more capable. In recent years, the integration of AI into edge devices has become increasingly prevalent, enabling real-time data processing and decision-making at the edge of the network.

One of the primary motivations for AI in edge computing is the need for low-latency responses in applications that demand immediate action, such as autonomous vehicles, industrial automation, and augmented reality. Edge devices, which can include sensors, cameras, smartphones, and IoT devices, benefit from AI algorithms that can process data locally without relying on distant data centers.

The deployment of AI models on edge devices requires the optimization of these models for resource-constrained environments, considering factors like power consumption, memory, and processing capabilities. This optimization often involves quantization, pruning, and model compression techniques to reduce the size of AI models while maintaining acceptable performance.

AI at the edge opens up a wide range of possibilities, from intelligent surveillance cameras that can identify objects and anomalies in real-time to autonomous drones that navigate complex environments without continuous connectivity to the cloud. These capabilities have applications in various industries, including agriculture, healthcare, manufacturing, and logistics.

Edge AI also plays a crucial role in edge computing for the Internet of Things (IoT). With billions of IoT devices generating vast amounts of data, processing this data locally using AI can help filter out irrelevant information and reduce the burden on centralized cloud servers.

Security and privacy are significant concerns in the deployment of AI at the edge. Edge devices often handle sensitive data, such as biometric information or industrial control systems, making it essential to implement robust security measures. AI can be used to enhance security by detecting anomalies and potential threats in real-time.

Federated learning is an emerging technique that allows AI models to be trained collaboratively across multiple edge devices while keeping data localized and private. This approach enables edge devices to collectively improve AI models without sharing sensitive data with a central server.

Edge devices with AI capabilities can also provide real-time insights and predictions, making them valuable tools in decision-making processes. For example, in agriculture, edge devices equipped with AI can monitor soil conditions, weather patterns, and crop health to optimize irrigation and crop management.

In the healthcare sector, wearable devices and medical sensors with AI can continuously monitor a patient's vital signs and alert medical professionals to potential issues, improving patient care and early intervention.

Manufacturing and industrial automation benefit from edge AI by enabling predictive maintenance of machinery. AI models can analyze sensor data from machines to detect signs of wear or malfunction, allowing maintenance teams to address issues proactively and minimize downtime.

Edge AI is also transforming the way we interact with technology through natural language processing (NLP) and computer vision. Voice assistants, such as smart speakers and virtual personal assistants, use edge AI to process spoken commands locally, providing quick responses without relying on cloud services.

Computer vision applications on edge devices enable augmented reality experiences, facial recognition, and object detection in real-time, enhancing user interfaces and improving security.

The development of edge AI requires a combination of hardware and software innovations. Specialized hardware accelerators, such as graphics processing units (GPUs) and tensor processing units (TPUs), are designed to perform AI inference efficiently on edge devices.

Edge AI frameworks and libraries, like TensorFlow Lite and PyTorch Mobile, enable the deployment of AI models on a wide range of edge devices and operating systems.

Edge computing and edge AI also have implications for the future of autonomous systems. Autonomous vehicles, drones, and robots rely on onboard AI to navigate and make decisions in real-time, reducing the need for constant connectivity to central servers.

In summary, AI in edge computing and edge devices is a transformative technology that brings intelligence to the edge of the network, enabling real-time processing, improved security, and more efficient use of resources. From healthcare to agriculture, manufacturing to autonomous systems, the integration of AI at the edge is shaping the future of technology and how we interact with the world around us.

BOOK 4
EXPERT NEURAL NETWORK PROGRAMMING: PUSHING
THE BOUNDARIES OF AI DEVELOPMENT WITH
ADVANCED PYTHON, TENSORFLOW, AND KERAS
TECHNIQUES

ROB BOTWRIGHT

Chapter 1: Reinventing Neural Network Architectures

Residual Networks, often referred to as ResNets, have emerged as a groundbreaking architectural innovation in deep learning that addresses the challenges of training very deep neural networks. The development of ResNets, which was awarded the prestigious Turing Award in 2018, has significantly contributed to the advancement of computer vision, natural language processing, and various other fields.

One of the fundamental problems in training deep neural networks is the issue of vanishing gradients. As a neural network becomes deeper, the gradients during backpropagation tend to get smaller and may eventually vanish, making it challenging to update the weights of early layers effectively.

ResNets tackle this problem by introducing skip connections, also known as residual connections or shortcut connections. These connections allow the gradient to flow directly from one layer to another without passing through a series of intermediate layers, mitigating the vanishing gradient problem.

The key innovation in ResNets is the residual block, which consists of a stack of convolutional layers followed by skip connections. These skip connections add the output of one layer to the output of another layer downstream, effectively creating a shortcut for the gradient to propagate.

In a residual block, the output of a layer is not just the result of the layer's computations but is also augmented by the residual, which is the difference between the output and the input. Mathematically, this is expressed as $F(x) = H(x) + x$, where $F(x)$ is the output of the residual block, $H(x)$ represents the layer's computations, and x is the input to the block.

This simple yet powerful architecture change allows for the training of extremely deep neural networks with hundreds or even thousands of layers. The gradient can propagate through the skip connections, allowing for the successful training of deep ResNets.

ResNets have had a profound impact on computer vision tasks, such as image classification and object detection. In the 2015 ImageNet Large Scale Visual Recognition Challenge, ResNets achieved remarkable results, outperforming previous models and reducing the top-5 error rate significantly.

One of the advantages of ResNets is their ability to learn both low-level and high-level features simultaneously. The skip connections enable the network to capture fine-grained details in early layers while also learning abstract representations in deeper layers.

ResNets have also been adapted to various other domains beyond computer vision. In natural language processing, for instance, Residual Recurrent Neural Networks (ResRNNs) have been proposed, which incorporate residual connections into recurrent layers, improving the training of deep sequence models.

Another notable feature of ResNets is their scalability. Researchers have developed different variants of ResNets, including Wide Residual Networks (Wide ResNets) and DenseNets, which further extend the architecture's capabilities.

Wide ResNets increase the width of residual blocks, which means they have more channels in each layer. This increased width enhances the model's representation power and can lead to improved performance, especially when dealing with small datasets.

DenseNets, short for Dense Convolutional Networks, take a different approach by connecting each layer to every other layer in a feedforward fashion. This dense connectivity ensures that each layer has access to the features learned in all preceding layers, promoting feature reuse and gradient flow.

ResNets have not only advanced the state of the art in deep learning but have also inspired new architectural ideas. Skip connections and residual connections have become a fundamental building block in designing deep neural networks.

The success of ResNets has also led to the development of variants tailored to specific tasks. For example, in semantic segmentation, Fully Convolutional Residual Networks (FCN-ResNets) have been designed to perform pixel-level labeling tasks, such as image segmentation.

Transfer learning with pre-trained ResNets has become a common practice in various domains. Researchers and practitioners can fine-tune pre-trained ResNets on their specific datasets, leveraging the learned representations from large-scale datasets like ImageNet.

Despite their numerous advantages, ResNets are not without challenges. Training very deep networks still requires careful initialization and regularization techniques to avoid issues like overfitting.

Furthermore, the design of ResNets may not be optimal for all tasks, and selecting the right architecture variant and hyperparameters is essential for achieving the best performance.

In summary, Residual Networks, or ResNets, have revolutionized the field of deep learning by addressing the vanishing gradient problem and enabling the training of extremely deep neural networks. Their skip connections, which allow the gradient to flow freely through layers, have led to significant improvements in computer vision and other domains. ResNets have set new benchmarks in various tasks and continue to inspire advancements in deep neural network architectures.

Capsule Networks, commonly known as CapsNets, represent a novel approach to deep learning architectures, designed to overcome some of the limitations of traditional convolutional neural networks (CNNs) in tasks like object recognition, pose estimation, and natural language processing.

The concept of CapsNets was introduced by Geoffrey Hinton and his colleagues in a 2017 paper titled "Dynamic Routing Between Capsules," and it has since garnered significant interest in the machine learning community.

Capsule Networks aim to address a fundamental problem in CNNs called "routing by agreement." In traditional CNNs, layers of neurons perform simple operations like convolutions and pooling to detect features, but the hierarchical relationships between these features are not explicitly represented.

CapsNets introduce the idea of capsules, which are groups of neurons that work together to represent a specific feature or entity in an image or text. These capsules allow for the explicit modeling of part-whole relationships and spatial hierarchies in data.

The primary building block of CapsNets is the capsule. A capsule is a small group of neurons, each responsible for detecting a specific feature within its receptive field. Capsules replace the traditional neurons in CNNs, and they are designed to capture richer information about an object's pose, deformation, and other characteristics.

In CapsNets, capsules are organized into multiple layers, much like the layers in CNNs. However, the crucial difference lies in how information flows between these layers.

Dynamic routing is a key mechanism in CapsNets that enables the flow of information between capsules. Instead of using fixed weights as in traditional CNNs, dynamic routing allows capsules to communicate with each other, forming consensus about the presence of particular features or objects.

Dynamic routing works by iteratively adjusting the coupling coefficients between capsules. Capsules in a higher-level layer send "votes" to capsules in the layer below, indicating their belief in the presence of a specific feature. The lower-level capsules then "weight" these votes based on their agreement with the predictions of the higher-level capsules.

Through this iterative process, capsules reach a consensus about the presence, pose, and other characteristics of objects in the input data. This dynamic routing by agreement enables CapsNets to handle complex hierarchical structures and spatial relationships.

Capsules are designed to encode not just the presence of features but also their pose information. This means that

CapsNets can recognize objects even when they appear in different orientations, sizes, or positions within an image.

One of the significant advantages of CapsNets is their potential for improved generalization. Traditional CNNs often require a large amount of labeled training data to perform well on new, unseen examples. In contrast, CapsNets can capture the underlying hierarchical structure of data, making them more robust to variations and distortions.

CapsNets have shown promising results in various applications. For instance, in image recognition tasks, CapsNets have demonstrated the ability to recognize objects even when they are occluded or appear at novel orientations. This has potential implications for robotics, autonomous vehicles, and augmented reality applications.

CapsNets have also shown promise in natural language processing. In tasks like sentiment analysis or question-answering, where understanding the context and relationships between words is crucial, CapsNets may offer a more effective approach compared to traditional models.

Despite their potential advantages, CapsNets are not without challenges. One limitation is the computational cost of dynamic routing, which can be expensive for deep networks. Efforts are ongoing to develop more efficient routing algorithms.

Additionally, the architectural design of CapsNets is still an active area of research. Researchers are exploring different capsule architectures, including variations that combine capsules with convolutional layers, recurrent networks, and attention mechanisms.

The success of CapsNets highlights the ongoing evolution of deep learning architectures. As machine learning researchers continue to explore novel approaches to modeling data, CapsNets represent an exciting step toward more interpretable and robust deep neural networks.

In summary, Capsule Networks, or CapsNets, offer a fresh perspective on deep learning by introducing capsules as building blocks that capture hierarchical relationships and pose information in data. Their dynamic routing mechanism enables consensus among capsules, making them suitable for complex tasks where spatial hierarchies are crucial. While challenges remain, CapsNets hold promise for improving the generalization and interpretability of deep neural networks across various domains.

Chapter 2: Advanced Optimizers and Learning Rate Schedules

In the realm of optimization algorithms for training neural networks, two prominent choices are the Adam optimizer and the RMSprop optimizer, each with its unique characteristics and advantages.

The Adam optimizer, short for Adaptive Moment Estimation, is an optimization algorithm that combines the benefits of two other popular optimizers: the RMSprop and momentum methods. This hybrid approach aims to address some of the limitations of these individual techniques.

One of the key features of the Adam optimizer is its adaptability to the learning rate. It dynamically adjusts the learning rate for each parameter during training, allowing it to handle different types of data and model architectures effectively.

The algorithm maintains two moving averages for each parameter in the network: the first moment (mean) and the second moment (uncentered variance). These moving averages are computed using exponential decay, and they help Adam adaptively scale the learning rates.

The first moment, often referred to as the "momentum" term, helps the optimizer build up velocity in the parameter updates, similar to the momentum optimizer. This helps Adam to navigate through flat or noisy parts of the loss landscape more efficiently.

The second moment, which can be thought of as a kind of "adaptive learning rate," helps Adam to scale the parameter updates. It makes smaller updates for parameters with smaller gradients and larger updates for parameters with larger gradients.

To prevent the moving averages from getting too biased initially, Adam applies a bias correction term. This bias correction ensures that the averages are more accurate, especially at the beginning of training.

One of the advantages of Adam is its ability to perform well on a wide range of deep learning tasks without requiring extensive manual tuning of hyperparameters. This adaptability to different tasks and architectures has made Adam a popular choice among machine learning practitioners.

However, there are situations where Adam may not be the best choice. For example, in some cases, Adam can converge faster but achieve a slightly worse final performance compared to other optimizers. This trade-off between speed and accuracy should be considered when selecting an optimizer for a specific task.

On the other hand, the RMSprop optimizer, short for Root Mean Square Propagation, is another optimization algorithm designed to address some of the limitations of traditional stochastic gradient descent (SGD). RMSprop adjusts the learning rates of individual parameters based on the historical gradient information.

In RMSprop, like Adam, each parameter has its own learning rate, which is adapted during training. The key insight behind RMSprop is to scale the learning rates inversely with the historical moving average of squared gradients for each parameter.

By doing so, RMSprop effectively handles the problem of vanishing or exploding gradients. It normalizes the updates based on the recent gradient history, preventing large updates that can hinder convergence.

RMSprop also incorporates an exponentially weighted moving average for the squared gradients, similar to the second moment in Adam. This moving average helps adjust the learning rates for each parameter adaptively.

One of the strengths of RMSprop is its simplicity. It requires fewer hyperparameters to be tuned compared to more complex optimizers like Adam. This can be advantageous when dealing with limited computational resources or when quick experimentation is necessary.

However, RMSprop, like other optimization algorithms, is not a one-size-fits-all solution. In some cases, it may converge slower or get stuck in suboptimal solutions compared to more advanced optimizers like Adam.

Choosing between Adam and RMSprop often depends on the specific task and the characteristics of the dataset. It is advisable to experiment with both optimizers and compare their performance on your particular problem.

In practice, it's worth noting that the default settings for Adam and RMSprop in popular deep learning frameworks like TensorFlow and PyTorch often work well for a wide range of tasks. However, fine-tuning the hyperparameters or trying alternative optimizers can sometimes lead to better results.

In summary, the Adam optimizer and the RMSprop optimizer are two widely used optimization algorithms in deep learning. Adam combines momentum and adaptive learning rates to adapt to different tasks and architectures, while RMSprop adapts learning rates based on the historical gradient information. Choosing between these optimizers depends on the specific requirements of your machine learning task, and experimentation is often key to finding the best optimizer for your needs. In the realm of deep learning, the choice of learning rate is a crucial hyperparameter that can significantly impact the training of neural networks. The learning rate determines the size of the steps taken during optimization and directly affects the convergence and performance of the model.

While selecting an appropriate learning rate is essential, it's not always a straightforward task. In practice, a fixed learning rate often encounters challenges, such as convergence issues or suboptimal performance.

To address these challenges, learning rate annealing strategies are employed to dynamically adjust the learning rate during training. These strategies aim to find a balance between fast convergence in the initial phases of training and stable convergence in the later phases.

One common learning rate annealing technique is known as learning rate scheduling. With learning rate scheduling, the learning rate is reduced over time in a predetermined manner.

A simple and widely used learning rate scheduling method is step decay. In step decay, the learning rate is reduced by a fixed factor after a predefined number of epochs. This approach allows the model to make larger steps in the initial training phases and gradually refine the weights as the training progresses.

For example, one might start with a learning rate of 0.1 and reduce it by a factor of 0.1 every 10 epochs. This way, the learning rate is annealed to 0.01 after 10 epochs, 0.001 after 20 epochs, and so on.

Another common learning rate scheduling technique is known as exponential decay. In exponential decay, the learning rate is reduced exponentially over time. The rate of decay is determined by a hyperparameter, often denoted as "decay factor" or "decay rate."

Exponential decay can be mathematically described as $lr(t) = lr0 * e^{(-kt)}$, where $lr(t)$ is the learning rate at time t, lr0 is the initial learning rate, k is the decay rate, and t is the current training step or epoch.

By adjusting the decay factor, one can control the rate at which the learning rate decreases. A larger decay factor results in a faster decrease, while a smaller one leads to a slower decrease.

Learning rate schedules are not limited to step decay and exponential decay. Other scheduling strategies, such as polynomial decay and cyclic learning rates, offer different ways to dynamically adjust the learning rate.

Polynomial decay involves reducing the learning rate as a function of the training progress. For example, one might use a polynomial of degree 2 to gradually decrease the learning rate, ensuring a smoother transition.

Cyclic learning rates, on the other hand, alternate between low and high learning rates during training. This approach encourages exploration of different regions of the loss landscape and can lead to improved convergence.

Aside from learning rate scheduling, another widely used learning rate annealing strategy is the learning rate finder method. In this approach, the learning rate is increased exponentially from a small value. During this phase, the model's loss is monitored to find the optimal learning rate range where it decreases steadily.

The learning rate finder method helps in identifying a suitable learning rate for training without the need for manual tuning. Once the optimal range is determined, one can then apply learning rate scheduling or other annealing techniques within that range.

While learning rate annealing strategies are effective in improving the convergence and performance of neural networks, it's essential to consider the specific characteristics of the task and dataset. Different tasks may benefit from different annealing methods, and experimentation is often necessary to find the most effective approach.

In practice, many deep learning frameworks, such as TensorFlow and PyTorch, provide built-in support for various learning rate annealing strategies. These frameworks make it easier for practitioners to implement and experiment with different annealing techniques.

In summary, learning rate annealing strategies play a crucial role in training deep neural networks effectively. By dynamically adjusting the learning rate during training, these strategies help address challenges like convergence issues and suboptimal performance. Learning rate scheduling, learning rate finder methods, and other annealing techniques offer valuable tools for fine-tuning the training process and improving the overall performance of deep learning models.

Chapter 3: Custom Training Loops and Gradient Tape

In the world of deep learning, loss functions are a fundamental component of the training process for neural networks. These functions quantify the error or deviation between the model's predictions and the actual target values, providing a crucial signal for adjusting the model's parameters during training.

While many standard loss functions are readily available for various machine learning tasks, there are situations where custom loss functions are necessary. Custom loss functions allow you to tailor the optimization process to the specific requirements of your problem, often leading to improved model performance.

The need for custom loss functions arises when the standard loss functions do not adequately capture the nuances of the problem you're trying to solve. Standard losses like mean squared error (MSE) or categorical cross-entropy are versatile and work well in many cases, but they might not be the best fit for every scenario.

One common scenario where custom loss functions are beneficial is when dealing with imbalanced datasets. In classification tasks with imbalanced classes, standard loss functions can favor the majority class, leading to suboptimal performance on the minority class. Custom loss functions can be designed to give more weight to the minority class, addressing this imbalance and improving overall model performance.

Another scenario where custom loss functions shine is in tasks with specific constraints or requirements. For instance, in anomaly detection, where the goal is to identify rare events, a custom loss function can be tailored to focus on minimizing false positives while allowing for more false negatives.

Implementing a custom loss function typically involves defining a mathematical expression that quantifies the error or discrepancy between the model's predictions and the ground truth. This expression should reflect the specific objectives and constraints of your problem.

In deep learning frameworks like TensorFlow or PyTorch, you can easily create custom loss functions by defining them as Python functions. These functions take the model's predictions and the ground truth as inputs and return a scalar value representing the loss.

Let's consider an example of a custom loss function for a regression task where the goal is to predict a target variable with an upper and lower bound. In this case, you could create a custom loss that penalizes predictions that fall outside the specified bounds more heavily.

To implement such a custom loss function in TensorFlow, you might write a Python function like this:

```
pythonCopy code
import tensorflow as tf def custom_loss(y_true, y_pred): lower_bound = 0 # Replace with your lower bound upper_bound = 1 # Replace with your upper bound # Calculate the error between predictions and ground truth error = y_pred - y_true # Clip the error to ensure it falls within the bounds clipped_error = tf.clip_by_value(error, lower_bound, upper_bound) # Calculate the squared error squared_error = tf.square(clipped_error) # Calculate the mean squared
```

error as the final loss loss = tf.reduce_mean(squared_error) return loss

In this example, the **custom_loss** function first calculates the error between predictions (**y_pred**) and ground truth (**y_true**). It then clips the error to ensure it falls within the specified bounds to prevent extreme errors from dominating the loss.

After clipping, it calculates the squared error and takes the mean to obtain the final loss value. This custom loss function places more emphasis on penalizing errors outside the bounds, aligning it with the specific requirements of the problem.

Once you've defined your custom loss function, you can use it as the loss metric when compiling your neural network model. For example, in TensorFlow, you can compile your model like this:

pythonCopy code

```
model.compile(optimizer='adam', loss=custom_loss)
```

Now, during training, the model will optimize its parameters to minimize the custom loss you've defined, taking into account the problem-specific constraints and objectives.

Custom loss functions offer a powerful way to fine-tune the training process and adapt it to the unique characteristics of your machine learning problem. They allow you to express your problem's requirements mathematically and guide the optimization process towards better results.

However, it's essential to keep in mind that designing custom loss functions requires a deep understanding of the problem and careful consideration of the trade-offs between different objectives. Experimentation and iterative refinement are often necessary to create an effective custom loss function that improves model performance.

In the ever-evolving field of deep learning, the training of neural networks often encounters challenges related to the size of the model, the amount of data available, and the computational resources required. To address these challenges, techniques like gradient accumulation and distributed training have become indispensable tools in the deep learning practitioner's toolkit.

Gradient accumulation is a technique used to combat the limitations of limited GPU memory during the training of large neural networks. In deep learning, backpropagation computes gradients for each batch of data processed during training and updates the model's parameters accordingly.

However, as models grow in size and complexity, the gradients themselves become larger, and storing all of them in GPU memory can be problematic. This issue can be particularly pronounced when training on high-resolution images, processing large text corpora, or working with massive datasets.

To tackle this problem, gradient accumulation allows for accumulating gradients over multiple mini-batches before performing a single update step. Instead of updating the model parameters after processing each mini-batch, the gradients are aggregated over several mini-batches and then applied as a single update.

The number of mini-batches over which gradients are accumulated is referred to as the accumulation step. For example, with an accumulation step of 4, gradients from four consecutive mini-batches are averaged, and this average is used to update the model's parameters.

This approach effectively reduces the memory requirements for gradient storage while still maintaining the benefits of mini-batch training, such as improved convergence and faster training.

To implement gradient accumulation, one can modify the training loop to accumulate gradients and perform parameter updates at specified intervals. In popular deep learning frameworks like TensorFlow and PyTorch, this can be achieved by accumulating gradients in a separate variable and applying updates after a defined number of accumulation steps.

For example, in TensorFlow, a custom training loop with gradient accumulation might look like this:

pythonCopy code

```python
import tensorflow as tf # Define your neural network model model = ... # Define optimizer and loss function optimizer = tf.keras.optimizers.Adam(learning_rate=0.001) loss_fn = ... # Set accumulation steps accumulation_steps = 4 # Initialize variables for accumulating gradients accumulated_gradients = [tf.Variable(tf.zeros_like(var)) for var in model.trainable_variables] # Training loop for epoch in range(num_epochs): for batch in dataset: with tf.GradientTape() as tape: logits = model(batch['input']) loss = loss_fn(batch['target'], logits) # Calculate gradients for this batch gradients = tape.gradient(loss, model.trainable_variables) # Accumulate gradients for i in range(len(gradients)):
```

```
accumulated_gradients[i].assign_add(gradients[i]         /
accumulation_steps) # Perform parameter update after
accumulation    steps    if    batch_counter    %
accumulation_steps              ==              0:
optimizer.apply_gradients(zip(accumulated_gradients,
model.trainable_variables))    #    Reset    accumulated
gradients  for  i  in  range(len(accumulated_gradients)):
accumulated_gradients[i].assign(tf.zeros_like(accumulate
d_gradients[i]))  batch_counter += 1  # End of epoch:
perform remaining updates if needed  if batch_counter %
accumulation_steps              !=              0:
optimizer.apply_gradients(zip(accumulated_gradients,
model.trainable_variables))         for        i        in
range(len(accumulated_gradients)):
accumulated_gradients[i].assign(tf.zeros_like(accumulate
d_gradients[i]))
```

In this example, gradients are accumulated over
accumulation_steps mini-batches, and parameter
updates are performed at regular intervals. This allows for
efficient training of large models with limited GPU
memory.

Distributed training, on the other hand, is a technique
used to leverage multiple GPUs or even multiple machines
to accelerate the training process. Deep learning models
can be computationally intensive, and training them on a
single GPU may not be practical for larger models or
datasets.

Distributed training distributes the computational
workload across multiple GPUs or machines, allowing for
parallel processing and faster training. This approach is

particularly beneficial for large-scale projects and deep learning research, where efficient resource utilization is crucial.

To implement distributed training, deep learning frameworks like TensorFlow and PyTorch provide libraries and tools that facilitate the distribution of computation across devices and machines. These libraries enable data parallelism, where each device or machine processes a portion of the training data and computes gradients independently.

For example, TensorFlow's **tf.distribute.Strategy** provides a high-level API for distributing training across multiple GPUs or TPUs. PyTorch offers similar capabilities through its **torch.nn.DataParallel** and **torch.nn.parallel.DistributedDataParallel** modules.

In distributed training, it's common to use synchronized gradient updates to ensure that all devices or machines have the most up-to-date model parameters. Synchronization can be achieved through methods like gradient averaging or gradient accumulation.

Overall, gradient accumulation and distributed training are essential techniques for overcoming the challenges posed by large models and massive datasets in deep learning. These techniques enable practitioners to train more complex models efficiently and make deep learning accessible for a broader range of applications.

Chapter 4: Distributed Training and Scalability

In the realm of training large and complex deep learning models, the distribution of computational workloads plays a pivotal role. Two fundamental strategies for distributing these workloads are data parallelism and model parallelism, each with its own advantages and trade-offs.

Data parallelism is a widely used technique in deep learning that focuses on distributing the training data across multiple devices or machines. The core idea behind data parallelism is to replicate the model on each device and train it with different subsets of the data, allowing for parallel processing.

This strategy is particularly effective when dealing with large datasets, as it enables faster training by dividing the data into smaller, manageable chunks. Each device processes its assigned data and computes gradients independently, which are then synchronized and averaged to update the model's parameters.

Data parallelism is relatively easy to implement in popular deep learning frameworks like TensorFlow and PyTorch, thanks to dedicated libraries and tools for distributed training. Commands like **tf.distribute.Strategy** in TensorFlow and **torch.nn.DataParallel** in PyTorch simplify the process of scaling up training to multiple GPUs or machines.

One of the key advantages of data parallelism is its simplicity and ease of use. It doesn't require significant modifications to the model architecture, and it can efficiently handle large datasets that might not fit into the memory of a single device.

However, data parallelism has limitations when it comes to models that don't fit within the memory of a single GPU. For such models, model parallelism becomes necessary.

Model parallelism, as the name suggests, focuses on distributing the model itself across multiple devices or machines. Instead of replicating the entire model on each device, different parts of the model are assigned to different devices, allowing for the training of extremely large models that wouldn't be feasible with data parallelism alone.

In model parallelism, each device is responsible for computing the forward and backward passes for its portion of the model. These devices communicate with each other to exchange intermediate results and synchronize gradients to update the model parameters.

Implementing model parallelism is more complex than data parallelism, as it requires careful partitioning of the model and coordination between devices. Deep learning frameworks provide tools like **torch.nn.parallel.DistributedDataParallel** in PyTorch and model partitioning libraries to facilitate model parallelism.

Model parallelism is particularly useful for training enormous models, such as those used in state-of-the-art natural language processing tasks, where the model's sheer size exceeds the memory capacity of a single GPU or machine.

One of the notable advantages of model parallelism is its ability to handle extremely large models and distributed memory efficiently. It allows deep learning researchers to push the boundaries of model size and complexity, leading to breakthroughs in various fields.

However, model parallelism introduces challenges related to communication and synchronization between devices. The increased complexity can make debugging and optimizing the training process more challenging.

In practice, a combination of data parallelism and model parallelism, known as hybrid parallelism, is often used to tackle large-scale deep learning tasks. Hybrid parallelism leverages the strengths of both techniques, distributing data across devices while also partitioning the model to accommodate memory constraints.

The choice between data parallelism and model parallelism depends on several factors, including the model's size, the dataset's size, available computational resources, and the specific deep learning problem. It's essential for deep learning practitioners to understand these strategies and their trade-offs to make informed decisions when designing and training complex models.

Ultimately, data parallelism and model parallelism are indispensable tools that enable the training of increasingly complex and large-scale deep learning models. As the field continues to advance, these techniques will play a crucial role in pushing the boundaries of what is possible in artificial intelligence and machine learning.

In the world of deep learning, scalability is a fundamental concern, and as models become larger and more complex, the need for distributed training frameworks becomes apparent. Distributed TensorFlow, developed by Google, and Horovod, an open-source framework developed by

Uber, are two powerful tools that address this need and enable the training of deep neural networks at scale.

Distributed TensorFlow is an extension of the popular TensorFlow deep learning framework, designed to distribute the training process across multiple devices or machines. It leverages the concept of data parallelism, where each device processes a portion of the training data and synchronizes gradients to collectively update the model's parameters.

The core idea behind Distributed TensorFlow is to replicate the model and training data across multiple devices or machines, allowing for parallel processing. Each device computes gradients independently, and then these gradients are aggregated and averaged to update the model.

To use Distributed TensorFlow, you can set up a cluster of machines and distribute the training workload using TensorFlow's **tf.distribute.Strategy** API. This API simplifies the process of distributed training by providing abstractions for distributed devices, communication, and synchronization.

Horovod, on the other hand, is an open-source framework that focuses on making distributed deep learning training accessible and efficient. It was developed by Uber Technologies and has gained popularity in the deep learning community for its ease of use and performance benefits.

Horovod is designed to work with popular deep learning frameworks like TensorFlow, PyTorch, and MXNet, making it versatile and applicable to a wide range of projects. Its core feature is ring-based communication, which minimizes communication overhead and maximizes training speed.

To use Horovod, you typically wrap your deep learning model with a few lines of code, and Horovod handles the distribution and synchronization of training across multiple devices or machines. This simplicity and compatibility with various frameworks have made Horovod a popular choice for distributed deep learning.

Both Distributed TensorFlow and Horovod excel in distributed training scenarios, but they have different strengths and trade-offs. Distributed TensorFlow is tightly integrated with the TensorFlow ecosystem and provides more extensive support for TensorFlow-specific features and libraries. If you are primarily working with TensorFlow, it may be the natural choice for your distributed training needs.

On the other hand, Horovod's simplicity and framework-agnostic approach make it a versatile option. It allows you to use the same distributed training code across multiple deep learning frameworks, which can be advantageous in research or industry settings where different frameworks may be in use.

When selecting between Distributed TensorFlow and Horovod, consider factors such as your existing deep learning framework, the complexity of your model, and your specific use case. Both frameworks are excellent choices for distributed training, and the decision may come down to which aligns better with your project's requirements and constraints.

It's worth noting that distributed training is not without its challenges. Synchronizing gradients, handling communication overhead, and debugging distributed code can be complex tasks. However, frameworks like Distributed TensorFlow and Horovod abstract many of these complexities, making distributed training more accessible to deep learning practitioners.

Additionally, distributed training can significantly accelerate the training of large neural networks. It allows you to leverage multiple GPUs or machines, reducing the time required to achieve state-of-the-art performance on various deep learning tasks.

As deep learning models continue to grow in size and complexity, the importance of distributed training frameworks like Distributed TensorFlow and Horovod will only increase. They enable researchers and engineers to tackle ambitious projects and push the boundaries of what is possible in artificial intelligence and machine learning.

Chapter 5: Hardware Acceleration with GPUs and TPUs

In the ever-evolving landscape of deep learning and artificial intelligence, GPU acceleration has emerged as a critical component that significantly enhances the speed and performance of training complex neural networks. At the heart of this acceleration is CUDA, a parallel computing platform and API developed by NVIDIA. CUDA, which stands for Compute Unified Device Architecture, has become the standard for leveraging the power of GPUs for a wide range of computational tasks, including deep learning.

To understand the significance of CUDA in the context of GPU acceleration, it's essential to first grasp the fundamental concepts of GPUs and parallel computing. Unlike traditional CPUs, which are optimized for general-purpose computing tasks and execute instructions sequentially, GPUs are designed to perform parallel computations on a massive scale.

A typical GPU consists of thousands of small processing cores, each capable of executing tasks concurrently. This parallel architecture makes GPUs exceptionally well-suited for tasks that can be broken down into many smaller, independent operations, such as matrix multiplications and convolutional operations that are prevalent in deep learning.

CUDA serves as the bridge between the high-level programming languages used by deep learning frameworks like TensorFlow, PyTorch, and CUDA-capable GPUs. It provides a programming model and a set of libraries that enable developers to harness the full computational power of GPUs for their specific tasks.

The heart of CUDA programming is writing kernel functions, which are small segments of code that are executed in parallel on the GPU. These kernel functions are designed to perform specific tasks and can be thought of as the building blocks of GPU-accelerated applications.

To write CUDA kernel functions, developers use a language that is similar to C and C++. CUDA extends these languages with additional features and syntax to facilitate parallelism, such as thread indices and memory management directives. This allows developers to express their algorithms in a way that can be effectively parallelized on the GPU.

One of the key benefits of CUDA is that it provides fine-grained control over how computations are distributed and executed on the GPU. Developers can specify the number of threads and blocks that execute a kernel function, allowing for customization to match the specific requirements of their algorithms.

CUDA also includes a set of libraries that accelerate common computational tasks, such as linear algebra operations (cuBLAS), Fast Fourier Transforms (cuFFT), and sparse matrix operations (cuSPARSE). These libraries are highly optimized for GPU architectures and can significantly speed up deep learning workloads.

In addition to libraries, CUDA provides tools for memory management, profiling, and debugging, making it a comprehensive ecosystem for GPU programming. Profiling tools like NVIDIA's nvprof allow developers to analyze the performance of their CUDA applications and identify bottlenecks or areas for optimization.

CUDA's memory management system is crucial for efficient GPU programming. It includes different types of memory, such as global memory, shared memory, and constant memory, each with its own characteristics and use cases. Proper memory management is essential for optimizing GPU performance and avoiding memory-related issues like bottlenecks or out-of-memory errors.

To develop CUDA applications, developers typically use development environments provided by NVIDIA, such as NVIDIA CUDA Toolkit and NVIDIA Nsight, which integrate with popular IDEs like Visual Studio and support various operating systems, including Windows, Linux, and macOS.

While CUDA has become the de facto standard for GPU acceleration in deep learning, it's important to note that other GPU programming languages and frameworks exist. OpenCL, for example, is an open-standard framework for heterogeneous computing that can target a broader range of hardware, including GPUs, CPUs, and FPGAs. However, CUDA remains the most widely adopted and well-supported choice in the deep learning community due to NVIDIA's dominance in the GPU market and its active development and support for CUDA.

In recent years, GPU acceleration with CUDA has been instrumental in advancing the field of deep learning. It has enabled researchers and engineers to train larger and more complex neural networks, significantly reducing training times for state-of-the-art models. Deep learning frameworks like TensorFlow and PyTorch seamlessly integrate CUDA support, allowing practitioners to leverage GPUs without having to write low-level CUDA code themselves.

The impact of CUDA on deep learning goes beyond just faster training times. It has democratized access to powerful computing resources, making it possible for researchers and developers to experiment with and advance the state of the art in artificial intelligence. CUDA has fueled innovation in computer vision, natural language processing, reinforcement learning, and many other subfields of AI by enabling the rapid development and training of cutting-edge models.

As the field of deep learning continues to evolve, CUDA will likely remain a fundamental technology that empowers researchers and engineers to tackle increasingly complex and ambitious AI projects. Its role in GPU acceleration is not limited to deep learning but extends to various scientific and computational disciplines where parallelism and high-performance computing are essential.

In the realm of cloud-based artificial intelligence and deep learning, Tensor Processing Units, or TPUs, have emerged as specialized hardware accelerators designed to enhance the performance of machine learning workloads. TPUs are developed by Google and have been optimized for tasks involving large-scale neural network inference and training. These custom-designed processors have become an integral part of Google Cloud's infrastructure, allowing developers and organizations to harness their power for a wide range of AI applications.

TPUs are particularly well-suited for the demands of deep learning tasks, which often involve training and running neural networks with millions or even billions of parameters. Deep learning models have rapidly grown in size and complexity, necessitating hardware that can keep up with the computational requirements.

One of the key features of TPUs is their ability to deliver high computational throughput while maintaining energy efficiency. TPUs are designed with a focus on accelerating matrix operations, which are at the core of many neural network computations. This specialization allows TPUs to perform these operations significantly faster than traditional CPUs or GPUs.

To utilize TPUs in the cloud, developers can leverage Google Cloud's TPU offerings, which provide access to TPU resources on a pay-as-you-go basis. Google's cloud infrastructure seamlessly integrates TPUs into its ecosystem, making it relatively straightforward for users to harness their power.

Developers can train and deploy deep learning models on TPUs using popular machine learning frameworks such as TensorFlow. TensorFlow has built-in support for TPUs, allowing users to write their deep learning code and then target TPUs for acceleration with minimal modifications. This ease of integration has contributed to the widespread adoption of TPUs for cloud-based machine learning tasks.

When using TPUs in the cloud, users can choose from a variety of TPU types, each optimized for different workloads. These options include Cloud TPU v3, Cloud TPU v4, and more. The choice of TPU type depends on the specific requirements of the deep learning project, such as model size, training speed, and budget constraints.

While TPUs excel at accelerating deep learning workloads, they are not limited to training neural networks. TPUs can also be used for inference tasks, where models make predictions or classifications based on input data. This versatility makes TPUs a valuable resource for a wide range of AI applications, including image recognition, natural language processing, recommendation systems, and more.

In addition to their computational prowess, TPUs are designed to be highly scalable. Users can access multiple TPUs simultaneously to train models more quickly or handle larger datasets. This scalability is particularly valuable for organizations with intensive machine learning needs, as it allows them to distribute workloads efficiently across multiple TPUs.

Google Cloud provides comprehensive documentation and tutorials on how to leverage TPUs effectively for machine learning tasks. This educational material covers topics such as setting up TPU instances, optimizing code for TPUs, and maximizing performance during training and inference.

TPUs have played a pivotal role in advancing the field of deep learning. They have enabled researchers and organizations to train larger and more sophisticated models, leading to breakthroughs in areas like computer vision, natural language understanding, and reinforcement learning. The availability of TPUs in the cloud has democratized access to these powerful hardware accelerators, allowing a broader community of developers and researchers to take advantage of their capabilities.

The use of TPUs in the cloud has also been instrumental in addressing some of the challenges associated with the rapid growth of AI. With the ability to scale computational resources on-demand, organizations can tackle projects that were once deemed impractical due to the sheer amount of computation required. This scalability ensures that AI innovations continue to progress at a rapid pace.

TPUs are not limited to cloud-based deployments; they can also be used in on-premises environments for organizations with specific data security and compliance requirements. Google offers TPU hardware for purchase, enabling businesses to build their own on-premises TPU clusters for AI workloads.

In summary, Tensor Processing Units (TPUs) in the cloud have revolutionized the landscape of deep learning and artificial intelligence. These specialized hardware accelerators, developed by Google, offer high computational throughput and energy efficiency, making them ideal for training and inference tasks involving large-scale neural networks. With seamless integration into Google Cloud's ecosystem and support from popular machine learning frameworks like TensorFlow, TPUs have become a valuable resource for developers and organizations looking to accelerate their AI applications. Their scalability, versatility, and impact on AI research and innovation make TPUs a significant asset in the pursuit of advancing artificial intelligence.

Chapter 6: Federated Learning and Privacy-Preserving AI

In the ever-evolving landscape of distributed machine learning and privacy-preserving AI, federated averaging and secure aggregation have emerged as crucial techniques that address the challenges of training models on decentralized data sources while preserving data privacy and security. These techniques have gained prominence in scenarios where data is sensitive, such as in healthcare, finance, and personal devices, and organizations need to collaborate on machine learning models without sharing raw data.

Federated averaging is a decentralized machine learning approach that allows multiple parties or devices to collaboratively train a global model while keeping their data localized and private. It operates under the principle that data remains on the edge devices or within individual organizations, and only model updates are shared for aggregation.

The process of federated averaging typically begins with the selection of a global model architecture that all participating parties agree upon. Each party then independently trains the global model on its local data while maintaining strict privacy measures. Once local training is complete, these parties communicate only the model updates or gradients to a central server, which aggregates the updates to compute a new global model.

Federated averaging employs various aggregation methods, with the most common being simple weighted averaging, where each party's model update is weighted according to its contribution. This ensures that parties with more data or higher quality data have a greater influence on the global model. The aggregated model is then sent back to the parties for further local training and iteration.

One of the key advantages of federated averaging is its privacy-preserving nature. Since raw data remains decentralized and never leaves the local devices or organizations, sensitive information is protected. This makes federated averaging suitable for applications where data privacy regulations, such as GDPR in Europe or HIPAA in healthcare, must be adhered to.

Secure aggregation techniques play a crucial role in federated averaging by ensuring that the process of aggregating model updates is done in a way that conceals the individual updates from the central server. This prevents the central server from learning sensitive information about the local datasets.

One widely used secure aggregation technique is based on cryptographic protocols, such as secure multi-party computation (MPC). MPC allows parties to jointly compute functions over their inputs while keeping those inputs private. In the context of federated averaging, MPC enables the aggregation of model updates without revealing any party's update to the others.

Another approach to secure aggregation is differential privacy, a concept that adds carefully crafted noise to the model updates before aggregation. This noise ensures that the aggregated result does not reveal information about any specific update. While differential privacy provides strong privacy guarantees, it may introduce additional challenges in terms of model accuracy and convergence.

Federated averaging and secure aggregation have been applied in various real-world scenarios. For example, in the healthcare domain, hospitals can collaborate on training machine learning models to improve patient care without sharing sensitive patient data. Similarly, federated learning techniques can be used in financial institutions for fraud detection and risk assessment, where customer data remains confidential.

However, federated learning is not without its challenges. Communication overhead can be a significant issue, especially when parties have limited bandwidth or unreliable connections. The process of transmitting model updates to a central server and receiving aggregated models can consume substantial network resources.

Additionally, ensuring the security of federated learning systems is a complex task. Secure aggregation techniques need to be carefully implemented and continually updated to mitigate potential vulnerabilities and attacks.

Despite these challenges, federated averaging and secure aggregation represent critical advancements in the field of distributed machine learning. They enable organizations and individuals to collaborate on machine learning projects while safeguarding sensitive data. As privacy concerns continue to grow, federated learning techniques will play an increasingly vital role in facilitating secure and privacy-preserving AI collaborations across various domains.

Chapter 7: Quantum Neural Networks and Exotic Architectures

In the realm of cutting-edge technology and computational possibilities, quantum computing stands as a paradigm-shifting frontier, promising to revolutionize the way we perform complex computations. Quantum gates are at the heart of this transformative technology, serving as the fundamental building blocks that manipulate quantum bits, or qubits, in ways that classical bits could never achieve.

Quantum computing harnesses the principles of quantum mechanics, a branch of physics that governs the behavior of particles at the quantum scale. Unlike classical computers, which rely on bits that can represent either a 0 or a 1, quantum computers use qubits that can exist in multiple states simultaneously due to a property known as superposition.

Superposition allows quantum computers to explore many possible solutions to a problem simultaneously, offering the potential for exponential speedup in certain computational tasks. This advantage becomes even more pronounced when combined with another quantum property called entanglement, where the state of one qubit becomes correlated with the state of another, regardless of the distance separating them.

Quantum gates are analogous to classical logic gates in traditional computers but operate on qubits in ways that exploit their quantum properties. While classical logic gates perform logical operations like AND, OR, and NOT, quantum gates perform unitary transformations that can manipulate qubits in ways that classical gates cannot replicate.

One of the fundamental quantum gates is the quantum NOT gate, often denoted as the X gate. It flips the state of a qubit, changing a $|0\rangle$ state to a $|1\rangle$ state and vice versa. This basic operation serves as the foundation for more complex quantum gates and quantum circuits.

The quantum Hadamard gate, denoted as the H gate, is another crucial component of quantum computing. It introduces superposition by taking a $|0\rangle$ state to an equal superposition of $|0\rangle$ and $|1\rangle$ states. When applied to a qubit, the H gate places it in a state that is a combination of both 0 and 1 with equal probability, a property essential for many quantum algorithms.

Quantum gates can be combined to create quantum circuits, which are analogous to the logical circuits in classical computing. These circuits manipulate qubits to perform computations or solve problems that would be infeasible for classical computers due to their exponential complexity.

In addition to the X and H gates, there are several other important quantum gates, such as the Pauli gates (X, Y, and Z), the CNOT gate (controlled-NOT), the T gate, and the S gate. Each of these gates plays a specific role in quantum circuits and algorithms, allowing for a rich and versatile computational landscape.

Quantum algorithms, such as Shor's algorithm and Grover's algorithm, leverage the unique properties of quantum gates to perform tasks that are practically impossible for classical computers. Shor's algorithm, for instance, can factor large numbers exponentially faster than the best-known classical algorithms, posing a potential threat to modern cryptography.

Grover's algorithm, on the other hand, accelerates the search of an unsorted database, offering a quadratic speedup compared to classical search algorithms. This capability has implications for optimization problems and database searches in various fields.

The development of practical and scalable quantum computers is still in its early stages, with significant challenges to overcome, such as qubit stability, error correction, and decoherence. Building quantum gates and circuits that are both reliable and scalable is a formidable engineering task that requires precise control at the quantum level.

Quantum gates are also subject to quantum noise and environmental factors that can introduce errors into quantum computations. Error correction techniques, such as quantum error-correcting codes and fault-tolerant quantum computing, are active areas of research aimed at addressing these challenges.

One of the promising technologies in the realm of quantum gates is superconducting qubits, which are fabricated from superconducting materials and can be manipulated using microwave pulses. These qubits can be controlled with high precision and are the basis for many quantum processors developed by leading companies and research institutions.

Another approach to quantum computing involves trapped-ion qubits, where individual ions are held in electromagnetic traps and manipulated using lasers. Trapped-ion quantum computers have demonstrated long qubit coherence times and high-fidelity quantum gates, making them a strong contender in the quest for practical quantum computation.

Quantum gates and quantum computing hold the potential to transform fields ranging from cryptography and optimization to drug discovery and materials science. Quantum supremacy, the point at which quantum computers outperform classical computers on certain tasks, is an ongoing pursuit that will mark a significant milestone in the field.

As quantum technology continues to advance, the development of quantum algorithms, quantum gates, and quantum circuits will play a pivotal role in realizing the full potential of quantum computing. With ongoing research and innovation, we are on the cusp of an era where quantum computers may unlock solutions to complex problems that were previously deemed unsolvable, revolutionizing industries and our understanding of computation itself. In the quest for more efficient and brain-inspired forms of computing, neuromorphic computing has emerged as a fascinating and promising field that seeks to mimic the neural architecture of the brain. At the heart of neuromorphic computing are spiking neural networks, a class of artificial neural networks that aim to replicate the way neurons communicate in the brain through discrete electrical pulses or spikes.

Neuromorphic computing draws inspiration from the remarkable efficiency and capabilities of the human brain, which can perform complex cognitive tasks with remarkable energy efficiency compared to traditional von Neumann architecture-based computers. While conventional computers use binary logic gates and perform calculations sequentially, the brain employs parallel processing, fault tolerance, and adaptability, all of which contribute to its remarkable computational prowess.

Spiking neural networks, also known as SNNs, stand as a key pillar of neuromorphic computing and represent a fundamental departure from traditional artificial neural networks, such as feedforward and recurrent neural networks. Instead of continuous-valued activations and weighted connections, SNNs rely on discrete spikes, or action potentials, to convey information.

In the brain, neurons communicate through spikes, which are brief electrical pulses generated when the membrane potential of a neuron exceeds a certain threshold. These spikes travel along the axons of neurons and initiate further spikes in connected neurons through synapses, forming complex networks of information processing.

Spiking neural networks aim to capture this intricate communication process by modeling neurons as nodes that generate spikes and synapses as connections that transmit them. Unlike traditional neural networks, where computations are continuous and differentiable, SNNs operate in discrete time steps, and their state is determined by the timing of spikes.

One of the key advantages of spiking neural networks is their potential for ultra-low power consumption, making them highly suitable for edge computing and resource-constrained environments. This efficiency arises from the fact that SNNs primarily consume power when spikes occur, as opposed to continuous processing in traditional neural networks.

Furthermore, SNNs have demonstrated the capacity to handle spatiotemporal information effectively, making them well-suited for tasks involving time-varying data, such as sensory perception, gesture recognition, and event-based vision. The temporal precision of spikes allows SNNs to encode information in a manner that aligns with the natural temporal dynamics of the real world.

Training spiking neural networks, however, presents distinct challenges compared to conventional artificial neural networks. Gradient-based optimization techniques, such as backpropagation, which are widely used in training traditional neural networks, are not directly applicable to SNNs due to the non-differentiable nature of spike events.

As a result, researchers have developed various methods for training SNNs, including surrogate gradient methods, which approximate the gradients of spiking neurons in a way that enables gradient-based optimization. These approaches have made it possible to train deep spiking neural networks capable of performing complex tasks.

One prominent area where spiking neural networks have shown promise is in neuromorphic hardware and hardware-accelerated neuromorphic computing. Neuromorphic hardware aims to build specialized chips or devices that can efficiently simulate SNNs in real time, mimicking the parallelism and efficiency of the human brain.

Neuromorphic hardware often leverages the event-driven nature of SNNs, where computations only occur when spikes are generated, leading to substantial energy savings. Examples of neuromorphic hardware platforms include IBM's TrueNorth, SpiNNaker, and the BrainScaleS system, all of which aim to accelerate the adoption of neuromorphic computing in various applications.

One of the fascinating aspects of spiking neural networks is their potential for neuromorphic vision systems, which can process visual information with high efficiency and low latency. These systems can find applications in robotics, autonomous vehicles, and even prosthetic devices, where real-time perception and decision-making are critical.

Spiking neural networks have also gained traction in the field of neurobiology and neuroscience. They serve as a valuable tool for modeling and simulating the behavior of biological neurons and networks, helping researchers gain insights into the brain's functioning and behavior.

While spiking neural networks offer numerous advantages in terms of energy efficiency and temporal processing, they are not without their challenges. Developing efficient algorithms, training techniques, and hardware platforms for SNNs remains an active area of research, and achieving the full potential of neuromorphic computing requires overcoming these hurdles.

In summary, neuromorphic computing and spiking neural networks represent a promising frontier in the quest for more brain-like and energy-efficient computing systems. By emulating the way neurons communicate through discrete spikes, SNNs offer the potential to revolutionize fields such as robotics, neuroscience, edge computing, and more, ushering in an era of efficient and brain-inspired artificial intelligence. The journey toward harnessing the full power of spiking neural networks continues, driven by the pursuit of more efficient and capable computing paradigms inspired by the human brain.

Chapter 8: Ethical AI and Bias Mitigation Strategies

Ensuring fairness in machine learning is a critical and complex endeavor that has garnered increasing attention in recent years. As machine learning algorithms play a growing role in various aspects of our lives, from hiring decisions to lending practices and criminal justice, it's essential to address and mitigate the biases and unfairness that can emerge from these systems.

Fairness in machine learning is not a new concern, but advancements in technology have amplified both the potential for bias and the opportunities for addressing it. The goal of fairness in this context is to ensure that machine learning models and algorithms do not discriminate against individuals or groups based on their protected attributes, such as race, gender, age, or ethnicity.

To achieve fairness in machine learning, one must start by recognizing that bias can manifest in multiple ways throughout the machine learning pipeline. It can occur in data collection, data labeling, model training, and even in the interpretation and application of results. Thus, addressing bias requires a multifaceted approach.

Data collection is the first stage where fairness issues can arise. Biased or unrepresentative data can lead to skewed model outcomes. For instance, if a dataset used to train a hiring algorithm contains a historical bias towards hiring men for certain roles, the algorithm may perpetuate that bias, unfairly favoring male candidates.

To mitigate this, it's crucial to carefully curate and preprocess datasets, removing any biased or sensitive attributes. Additionally, techniques such as data augmentation and oversampling can be employed to ensure balanced representation of different groups.

Data labeling is another stage where fairness can be compromised. Human annotators might inadvertently introduce their own biases when labeling data. For example, in image recognition tasks, annotators may mislabel images of people from underrepresented groups more frequently, leading to a biased training dataset.

Addressing this challenge requires clear guidelines for annotators, continuous monitoring, and auditing of labeled data, and potentially using multiple annotators to reduce individual bias.

The model training process itself can introduce bias if not managed carefully. Traditional machine learning algorithms are designed to minimize errors, which can inadvertently amplify bias if the training data is biased. In the pursuit of accuracy, the model may predict outcomes that are biased against certain groups.

To counter this, fairness-aware machine learning techniques have emerged. These methods aim to incorporate fairness constraints into the training process, penalizing models for making biased predictions. Fairness constraints can take various forms, such as demographic parity or equalized odds, depending on the specific fairness goals.

Post-training fairness interventions are another approach to address bias. These techniques involve modifying the model's predictions or outcomes after it has been trained to ensure fairness. For example, a post-processing algorithm could adjust the model's predictions to achieve demographic parity.

It's important to note that fairness interventions can sometimes introduce trade-offs between fairness and accuracy. Striking the right balance between these competing objectives is a key challenge in fairness-aware machine learning.

In the real world, fairness considerations extend beyond the training phase. Deployed machine learning models can have unintended consequences, impacting people's lives and well-being. For example, a biased loan approval model could unfairly deny loans to minority applicants, perpetuating economic disparities.

To address this, it's essential to monitor the real-world impact of machine learning models and conduct regular audits to identify and rectify any unfairness. This ongoing evaluation is crucial to ensure that the model's behavior aligns with fairness goals.

Interpretability and transparency also play a vital role in fairness. Understanding why a model made a particular decision, especially when it involves sensitive attributes, is essential for accountability and fairness. Various techniques, such as model explanations and interpretable machine learning, can help shed light on model decision-making processes.

Furthermore, fairness is a multifaceted concept that encompasses both statistical and ethical dimensions. While statistical fairness aims to achieve balance and equality in outcomes, ethical considerations are equally important. Ethical fairness involves respecting individual rights, dignity, and avoiding discrimination based on protected attributes.

Legal and regulatory frameworks are also evolving to address fairness in machine learning. Laws like the

General Data Protection Regulation (GDPR) and the Equal Credit Opportunity Act (ECOA) place responsibilities on organizations to ensure fairness and transparency in their use of machine learning.

In summary, fairness in machine learning is a complex and multifaceted challenge that requires careful attention throughout the machine learning pipeline. From data collection and labeling to model training and deployment, addressing bias and ensuring fairness is an ongoing process that combines technological advancements, ethical considerations, and legal compliance. Achieving fairness in machine learning is not just an option; it's an ethical and societal imperative as we increasingly rely on these systems to make decisions that impact individuals and communities.

Bias detection and mitigation techniques are fundamental components of responsible and ethical machine learning. In an age where machine learning models are used in critical decision-making processes across various domains, it is imperative to ensure that these models do not perpetuate or amplify biases present in the data they are trained on. This chapter will explore the various approaches and methods for detecting and mitigating bias in machine learning models.

Bias in machine learning can manifest in different forms and at different stages of the modeling process. It can stem from biased data collection, where the training data itself is skewed or unrepresentative of the real-world population. It can also arise during data preprocessing and feature selection, where certain attributes may be unintentionally favored or disfavored. Furthermore, bias can be introduced by the algorithmic choices made during model training, leading to discriminatory predictions and outcomes.

To address bias effectively, one must first be able to detect it. Bias detection techniques aim to uncover disparities or imbalances in model predictions across different groups, often with respect to protected attributes such as race, gender, or age. Fairness metrics are commonly used to quantify these disparities, providing a quantitative basis for assessing bias.

One widely used fairness metric is demographic parity, which measures whether a model's predictions are distributed equally among different demographic groups. If a model exhibits demographic parity, it implies that its predictions are not biased with respect to those demographics. However, achieving demographic parity may not always be appropriate or desirable, as it can ignore underlying differences in the data.

Another fairness metric is equalized odds, which evaluates whether the model's predictions are equally accurate for all groups, irrespective of their protected attributes. Equalized odds is a stricter criterion than demographic parity, as it requires both true positive rates and false positive rates to be balanced across groups.

In addition to these fairness metrics, several bias detection tools and libraries have emerged in recent years to help practitioners identify and quantify bias in their machine learning models. Tools like IBM's AI Fairness 360 and Google's What-If Tool offer pre-built fairness metrics and visualization capabilities, making it easier to diagnose and understand bias in models.

Once bias has been detected, the next step is bias mitigation. Bias mitigation techniques aim to reduce or eliminate the disparities identified by fairness metrics while maintaining or improving the model's overall performance. Mitigation techniques can be broadly categorized into pre-processing, in-processing, and post-processing methods.

Pre-processing methods involve modifying the training data before it is used to train the model. One common approach is re-sampling, where the data is adjusted to ensure balanced representation across different groups. For instance, over-sampling can be applied to the minority group, while under-sampling can be used for the majority group. Another pre-processing technique is re-weighting the data, assigning different weights to different examples based on their protected attributes.

In-processing methods focus on adapting the model or the training process itself to mitigate bias. These methods often involve modifying the loss function used during training to include fairness constraints. For example, adversarial training introduces an additional adversarial network that aims to detect and penalize bias-inducing features in the model's representations.

Post-processing methods, as the name suggests, address bias after the model has been trained. They involve modifying the model's predictions to achieve fairness. One common post-processing approach is re-ranking, where the model's predictions are reordered to be fairer, often at the expense of prediction accuracy.

It's important to note that mitigating bias is not without challenges and trade-offs. Many bias mitigation techniques introduce a trade-off between fairness and model accuracy. Striking the right balance between these competing objectives is a key consideration when applying bias mitigation methods.

Moreover, fairness is not a one-size-fits-all concept. What is considered fair may vary depending on the specific domain and context. Different stakeholders may have different views on what constitutes fairness, making it essential to involve domain experts, ethicists, and impacted communities in the decision-making process.

Beyond technical solutions, addressing bias in machine learning also requires a holistic and interdisciplinary approach. Legal and regulatory frameworks, such as the General Data Protection Regulation (GDPR) in Europe and the Equal Credit Opportunity Act (ECOA) in the United States, place obligations on organizations to ensure fairness and transparency in their use of machine learning. Furthermore, ongoing monitoring and auditing of machine learning models in real-world settings are essential to identify and rectify any biases that may emerge over time. Regularly updating models with fresh data and refining fairness constraints can help maintain fairness in dynamic environments.

In summary, bias detection and mitigation are critical aspects of responsible machine learning. Detecting bias using fairness metrics and leveraging bias detection tools is the first step toward addressing it. Mitigating bias involves a range of techniques, from pre-processing and in-processing to post-processing methods, each with its own advantages and challenges. Achieving fairness in machine learning is an ongoing process that requires continuous attention, interdisciplinary collaboration, and a commitment to ethical principles and legal compliance.

As machine learning continues to shape our world, ensuring fairness in its applications is a collective responsibility that carries ethical, social, and legal significance.

Chapter 9: Interoperability and Model Deployment

Model serialization and compatibility are vital aspects of machine learning deployment and model management. Next, we delve into the intricacies of saving, loading, and ensuring compatibility for machine learning models, addressing the complexities of deploying models across different environments and platforms.

Machine learning models are the result of intricate training processes that involve optimizing thousands or even millions of parameters. These models encapsulate knowledge extracted from data and are essential for various applications, including recommendation systems, image classification, natural language processing, and more. To harness the power of these models, it's essential to understand how to serialize and deploy them effectively.

Serialization is the process of converting a complex data structure, such as a machine learning model, into a format that can be easily stored and transmitted. In the context of machine learning, serialization typically involves saving a trained model to a file or a format that can be used for later inference without the need to retrain the model.

One commonly used serialization format for machine learning models is the Python pickle format. Pickle allows you to serialize a Python object, including machine learning models, to a binary representation that can be saved to a file and later deserialized. While pickle is convenient for storing models in a Python-centric environment, it may not be the best choice when you need to share models across different programming languages or platforms.

A more widely adopted format for model serialization is the open-standard format, such as the ONNX (Open Neural Network Exchange) format. ONNX enables interoperability across different deep learning frameworks, allowing you to train a model in one framework and deploy it in another. This format has gained popularity due to its versatility and compatibility.

When saving a model using the ONNX format, you ensure that it can be easily loaded and utilized in various environments, including web applications, mobile devices, edge devices, and cloud platforms. This cross-platform compatibility simplifies the deployment process and widens the range of applications where your models can be employed.

However, compatibility doesn't stop at serialization formats. It extends to the libraries, frameworks, and hardware platforms on which your models are deployed. Ensuring compatibility across these dimensions is crucial for the seamless integration of machine learning models into real-world applications.

Library and framework compatibility involves making sure that the machine learning libraries and dependencies used during model training are consistent with those available in the deployment environment. For example, if you train a model using TensorFlow 2.0, you should ensure that the same or compatible version of TensorFlow is available when deploying the model. Incompatibilities between library versions can lead to unexpected behavior and errors during inference.

Hardware compatibility is another important consideration. Machine learning models can be deployed on a variety of hardware platforms, including CPUs, GPUs, and TPUs (Tensor Processing Units). Ensuring that your model can efficiently run on the target hardware requires optimizing the model's operations and utilizing hardware-specific libraries and tools when necessary.

A crucial aspect of hardware compatibility is edge deployment, where models run on resource-constrained devices such as IoT devices or edge servers. In edge computing scenarios, models often need to be optimized for lower power consumption, reduced memory usage, and faster inference times. This optimization can involve quantizing model weights, applying model pruning techniques, and leveraging hardware acceleration whenever possible.

Cross-platform compatibility also extends to the operating system and deployment environment. Whether your model is deployed on a Linux server, a Windows machine, or within a containerized environment like Docker, you need to ensure that the model can operate seamlessly without compatibility issues.

A crucial practice in achieving compatibility across these dimensions is version control and documentation. Keeping detailed records of the library versions, framework configurations, and hardware specifications used during model training is essential. This information serves as a reference point when deploying the model, ensuring that the same or compatible components are in place.

Furthermore, documentation is key to providing clear instructions for others who may need to deploy and use your models. Documentation should include guidance on model serialization formats, library dependencies, hardware requirements, and any specific deployment considerations. This documentation helps streamline the deployment process and avoids potential pitfalls.

Testing and validation are indispensable steps in ensuring model compatibility. Before deploying a model in a production environment, it's essential to rigorously test it in various deployment scenarios. This includes testing on different hardware platforms, operating systems, and deployment environments to identify and address compatibility issues early in the process.

Continuous integration and continuous deployment (CI/CD) pipelines can play a significant role in automating the testing and validation of model compatibility. By integrating model deployment into CI/CD pipelines, you can ensure that any changes to the model or its dependencies are thoroughly tested before they reach production environments.

Finally, monitoring and maintenance are ongoing activities in the lifecycle of deployed machine learning models. Even with thorough testing and validation, issues may arise in real-world deployments due to unforeseen changes or updates in the environment. Monitoring allows you to detect and address compatibility issues promptly, ensuring that the model continues to operate correctly.

In summary, model serialization and compatibility are critical considerations when deploying machine learning models. Choosing the right serialization format, ensuring compatibility across libraries, frameworks, and hardware platforms, and following best practices for documentation, testing, and monitoring are essential steps to deploy models successfully in diverse real-world scenarios. Achieving model compatibility paves the way for the effective and widespread use of machine learning in applications ranging from autonomous vehicles to healthcare and beyond.

Serving machine learning models in production is a crucial step in the deployment process. Once you have trained and serialized your model, you need to make it available for inference by serving it to clients or applications that require predictions. TensorFlow Serving, combined with containerization using Docker, offers a robust solution for serving machine learning models efficiently and reliably.

TensorFlow Serving is an open-source library developed by Google that is specifically designed for serving machine learning models in production. It provides a production-ready server environment that allows you to deploy models for online and batch prediction. TensorFlow Serving is particularly well-suited for serving models trained with TensorFlow, but it can also be used with other frameworks through TensorFlow's SavedModel format.

One of the key advantages of using TensorFlow Serving is its ability to handle model versioning and serving multiple models simultaneously. This enables you to seamlessly transition between different model versions, perform A/B testing, and gradually roll out updates to your models without disrupting service. Managing model versions in a systematic way is essential for maintaining the stability and reliability of your machine learning services.

Docker, on the other hand, is a platform for developing, shipping, and running applications inside containers. Containers are lightweight and portable, making them an ideal choice for packaging machine learning models and their serving environments. Docker containers encapsulate all the dependencies required to run your model, including the runtime libraries, system tools, and the model itself.

Combining TensorFlow Serving with Docker allows you to create containerized environments for serving machine learning models. This approach offers several benefits:

Isolation: Containers provide isolation from the host system, ensuring that your serving environment remains consistent regardless of the underlying infrastructure. This isolation prevents conflicts between different versions of system libraries or dependencies.

Portability: Docker containers are highly portable, allowing you to build a model-serving container on your development machine and then deploy it to various environments, such as cloud platforms, on-premises servers, or edge devices.

Scalability: Docker containers can be easily scaled horizontally to handle increased inference requests. You can use container orchestration tools like Kubernetes to manage and scale your model-serving containers dynamically.

Version Control: Docker images can be version-controlled and tagged, making it easy to track changes to your serving environment over time. You can also use container registries to store and distribute your Docker images.

To serve a machine learning model using TensorFlow Serving and Docker, you typically follow these steps:

Containerization: Create a Dockerfile that specifies the base image and includes instructions for installing the necessary dependencies and copying your serialized model into the container. Build the Docker image from the Dockerfile.

Deployment: Deploy the Docker image to your target environment. This could be a local machine, a cloud-based container service, or an edge device. Ensure that you have Docker installed on the deployment machine.

Serving Configuration: Configure TensorFlow Serving inside the container to load and serve your model. Specify the model version, input and output signatures, and any other serving-related settings.

Exposing Ports: In your Dockerfile or Docker run command, expose the ports required for communication with the TensorFlow Serving server. Typically, you expose ports for gRPC (used for model inference) and REST (used for management and monitoring).

Start Serving: Run the Docker container, which will start the TensorFlow Serving server. The server will load the model and listen for inference requests.

Client Integration: Develop or configure clients (applications or services) that send inference requests to the TensorFlow Serving server. Clients can use gRPC or REST APIs to interact with the server.

Monitoring and Scaling: Monitor the serving environment for performance, resource utilization, and errors. Use container orchestration tools to scale the serving containers based on demand.

Maintenance and Updates: As you develop new versions of your model, build and deploy updated Docker images with the new model versions. Follow best practices for managing model versions and updates.

TensorFlow Serving offers a range of features for managing the serving lifecycle, including model versioning, model introspection, and performance metrics monitoring. It also provides a RESTful API for administrative tasks, making it easier to manage and monitor your serving infrastructure.

Additionally, TensorFlow Serving supports model deployment on GPUs and TPUs, allowing you to take advantage of hardware acceleration for faster inference. This is especially important for deep learning models that require substantial computational resources.

In summary, serving machine learning models with TensorFlow Serving and Docker is a robust and versatile approach for deploying models in production. It offers the benefits of version control, portability, scalability, and isolation, making it well-suited for various deployment scenarios. By combining these technologies, you can ensure that your machine learning models are accessible, reliable, and performant in real-world applications.

Chapter 10: Future Frontiers in AI Research and Development

Explainable AI (XAI) and transparent machine learning (ML) are crucial aspects of modern artificial intelligence that address the need for understanding and interpreting the decisions made by AI systems. As AI technologies continue to advance and find applications in various domains, there is a growing concern about the "black box" nature of some models, where it can be challenging to comprehend how and why AI systems arrive at specific conclusions or predictions.

To address these concerns, researchers and practitioners have been working on developing methods and techniques for making AI models more interpretable and transparent. Explainable AI is the overarching field that encompasses these efforts and aims to provide insights into AI decision-making processes.

One of the primary motivations behind the push for XAI is accountability. When AI systems are used in critical domains such as healthcare, finance, and criminal justice, it is essential to have a clear understanding of why a particular decision was made. For instance, in a medical diagnosis system, it's not sufficient for the AI to say that a patient has a particular condition; doctors and patients need to know the reasoning behind that diagnosis.

Transparency in machine learning refers to the extent to which the inner workings of an AI model are accessible and understandable to humans. It involves making the model's architecture, parameters, and decision processes more open and comprehensible.

There are several techniques and approaches to achieving XAI and transparent ML:

1. Model Transparency: This approach involves designing machine learning models in a way that makes them inherently more interpretable. For example, using decision trees or linear models often produces results that are more straightforward to explain than complex deep neural networks.

2. Feature Importance: Understanding which features or variables had the most significant influence on a model's decision can provide insights into why a particular outcome was reached. Techniques like feature importance scores and partial dependence plots can help with this.

3. Local Interpretability: Local interpretability focuses on explaining specific model predictions for individual instances or cases. Methods such as LIME (Local Interpretable Model-agnostic Explanations) generate simplified models for explaining individual predictions.

4. Global Interpretability: Global interpretability aims to provide an overview of how the model behaves across its entire dataset. It includes techniques like SHAP (SHapley Additive exPlanations) values, which assign contributions to each feature for a model's output on a particular instance.

5. Rule-Based Models: Rule-based models, such as decision rules or production rules, provide a straightforward way to interpret AI decisions. These models consist of a set of rules that explicitly state how input features lead to output decisions.

6. Visualizations: Visualization techniques can help users understand AI model behavior by presenting data and decision boundaries graphically. For instance, heatmaps can illustrate the importance of different input features.

7. Ethical Considerations: Ensuring that AI systems are designed and used in an ethical manner is a crucial aspect of transparent ML. Ethical guidelines and principles can help guide the development and deployment of AI systems.

8. Regulatory Compliance: In some industries, there are regulatory requirements for transparency and explainability in AI systems. Compliance with these regulations is essential to avoid legal and ethical issues.

It's worth noting that achieving XAI and transparent ML can be a challenging task, especially for complex deep learning models. Balancing the trade-off between model performance and interpretability is an ongoing research area. Some techniques may reduce model complexity to enhance transparency but at the cost of accuracy.

Furthermore, the interpretability of AI systems is often domain-specific. What is considered an acceptable level of transparency may vary depending on the application. For instance, a recommendation system for online shopping may require less interpretability than a medical diagnostic tool.

In summary, explainable AI and transparent machine learning are essential for ensuring the responsible and ethical use of AI technology. They enable humans to understand, trust, and validate the decisions made by AI systems. While achieving complete transparency for all AI models is a complex challenge, ongoing research and the development of XAI techniques are making significant strides toward making AI more interpretable and accountable in various domains.

The intersection of bioinformatics and artificial intelligence (AI) has heralded a new era of innovation in healthcare, transforming the way we diagnose diseases, develop therapies, and understand the complexities of the human body. Bioinformatics, a multidisciplinary field that combines biology, computer science, and data analysis, plays a pivotal role in harnessing the power of AI to advance healthcare.

In recent years, there has been an explosion of biological data, from genomics and proteomics to medical imaging and electronic health records. This data deluge presents both a challenge and an opportunity. AI, with its capacity to analyze vast datasets and extract meaningful insights, has become indispensable in handling and interpreting this information.

One of the most profound applications of AI in bioinformatics is in genomics, where researchers use machine learning algorithms to decipher the human genome. Genomic sequencing, once an arduous and time-consuming task, has been accelerated and made more affordable through AI-driven techniques. This has opened the door to personalized medicine, where treatments can be tailored to an individual's genetic makeup.

AI-driven predictive modeling has also found its place in epidemiology and disease outbreak prediction. Machine learning algorithms can analyze patterns in disease data, helping public health officials prepare for and respond to epidemics more effectively. For instance, during the COVID-19 pandemic, AI models were used to forecast the spread of the virus and optimize resource allocation.

In the realm of drug discovery, AI has become a game-changer. Traditional drug development is costly and time-consuming, with a high failure rate. AI-driven drug discovery streamlines the process by identifying potential drug candidates and predicting their efficacy. This not only accelerates the development of new therapies but also reduces costs.

AI-powered image analysis is another area where bioinformatics and healthcare intersect. In medical imaging, machine learning algorithms can detect anomalies, such as tumors or fractures, with high accuracy. This aids radiologists in making faster and more accurate diagnoses. Furthermore, AI can analyze tissue samples at the cellular level, assisting in cancer diagnosis and treatment.

In addition to diagnostics and drug discovery, AI has revolutionized patient care. Electronic health records (EHRs) contain a wealth of patient data, but extracting useful information from them can be challenging. Natural language processing (NLP) algorithms can extract relevant clinical information from unstructured text, aiding in clinical decision support and improving patient outcomes.

Telemedicine has seen a surge in adoption, thanks in part to AI-powered chatbots and virtual assistants. These tools can provide patients with medical information, schedule appointments, and even offer mental health support, making healthcare more accessible and convenient.

Furthermore, AI-driven wearable devices can continuously monitor patients' vital signs and alert healthcare providers to any anomalies. This real-time data collection enables early intervention and better management of chronic conditions.

AI has also enhanced the field of drug repurposing, where existing drugs are investigated for new therapeutic uses. By analyzing large datasets, AI can identify potential candidates for repurposing, saving time and resources in drug development.

In genomics research, AI is not only used for sequencing but also for interpreting the data. It can identify genetic variants associated with diseases and predict an individual's risk. This information is invaluable in preventive medicine and personalized treatment plans.

Collaboration between researchers in bioinformatics and AI has led to the development of cutting-edge tools and platforms for analyzing biological data. These tools are essential for researchers working on projects such as the Human Cell Atlas, which aims to map all the cells in the human body, or the Cancer Genome Atlas, which explores the genetic basis of cancer.

Ethical considerations are paramount in the application of AI in healthcare and bioinformatics. Privacy concerns, data security, and potential biases in algorithms must be addressed to ensure that AI is used responsibly and equitably.

As AI continues to advance, the future of bioinformatics and healthcare looks promising. AI-driven innovations hold the potential to revolutionize disease diagnosis, treatment, and prevention, ultimately leading to improved patient outcomes and a healthier world.

In summary, the synergy between bioinformatics and AI has ushered in a new era of healthcare innovation. From genomics to drug discovery, diagnostics to patient care, AI is reshaping every aspect of the healthcare landscape. The ability to analyze vast datasets, make accurate predictions, and personalize treatments is transforming healthcare into a more efficient, accessible, and patient-centered field. With responsible implementation and ongoing research, the future holds even more exciting possibilities at the intersection of bioinformatics and AI in healthcare.

Conclusion

In this comprehensive bundle titled "Neural Network Programming: How to Create Modern AI Systems with Python, TensorFlow, and Keras," we embarked on a journey through the intricate world of artificial intelligence and deep learning. Across four meticulously crafted books, we explored the intricacies of neural network programming, from the fundamentals to the cutting-edge techniques that drive the future of AI development.

In Book 1, "Neural Network Programming for Beginners," we laid the foundation for understanding neural networks. Starting from scratch, we delved into the core concepts of AI, Python programming, and the TensorFlow and Keras frameworks. This book served as an entry point for newcomers, providing them with the essential knowledge to embark on their AI journey.

Book 2, "Advanced Neural Network Programming," took our readers on a deeper dive into the world of deep learning. With a solid understanding of the basics in place, we explored advanced techniques, fine-tuning models, and mastering the intricacies of TensorFlow and Keras. This book served as a bridge between the introductory concepts and the more advanced topics covered in the subsequent books.

In Book 3, "Neural Network Programming: Beyond the Basics," we pushed the boundaries of AI development by delving into advanced concepts and architectures. We explored convolutional neural networks (CNNs), recurrent neural networks (RNNs), generative adversarial networks (GANs), and more. This book equipped readers with the tools and knowledge to tackle complex AI projects and explore innovative AI solutions.

Finally, in Book 4, "Expert Neural Network Programming," we ventured into uncharted territories, where AI development knows no bounds. With advanced Python, TensorFlow, and Keras techniques at our disposal, we addressed quantum neural networks, ethical AI, model deployment, and glimpsed into the future of AI research and development. This book aimed to challenge and inspire AI enthusiasts and professionals to reach new heights in their AI endeavors.

As we conclude this journey through the world of neural network programming, we want to emphasize that AI is a continuously evolving field, and there is always more to explore and discover. These four books are your gateway to becoming proficient in neural network programming, from a beginner to an expert.

Whether you are just starting your AI journey, seeking to deepen your knowledge, or aiming to push the boundaries of AI development, this bundle has provided you with the essential tools, insights, and techniques. We hope that the knowledge you've gained here serves as a stepping stone for your AI projects, research, and innovations.

The field of AI is boundless, and the possibilities are endless. We encourage you to continue your exploration, collaborate with fellow enthusiasts, and contribute to the ever-growing landscape of artificial intelligence. Thank you for embarking on this journey with us, and may your future endeavors in neural network programming be both rewarding and transformative.